Scotland's Countryside Parks

Tom Prentice

Vol 1 – West

60 walks

In and around Scotland's Country Parks,

Country Estates & Regional Parks: Arran, Ayrshire,
As..... ....ber o.
In...   ...sgow, Clyde Valley, Stirling,

Dumfries & Galloway

*Finlaystone
Country Estate*

Contents

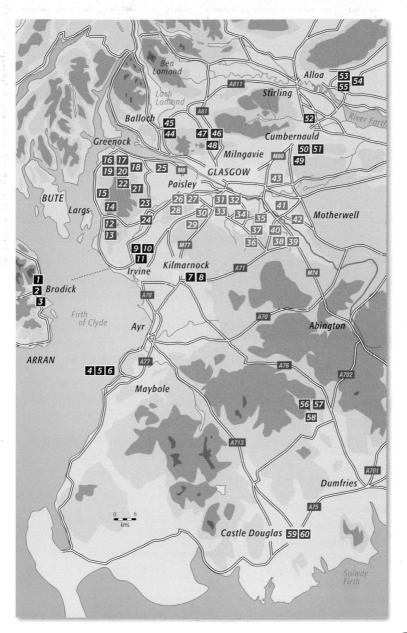

Ben Lomond

Loch Lomond

A811

Alloa

53 55 54

Stirling

River Forth

Balloch

A81

45 44

47 46

48

Cumbernauld

50 51 49

Greenock

Milngavie

16 17 18

25

M8

GLASGOW

19 20

22 21

43

15

Paisley

BUTE

14

23

26 27

31 32

41

Largs

24

28

30

33

34

35

Motherwell

12 13

29

37 40

42

9 10

36

38 39

11

M77

Kilmarnock

Irvine

7 8

A71

M74

1 2 3

Brodick

Firth of Clyde

A78

Ayr

A70

Abington

ARRAN

A77

4 5 6

A76

A702

Maybole

56 57 58

A713

Dumfries

A701

0   6
kms

A75

Castle Douglas 59 60

Solway Firth

3

Beside the Lugton Water,
Eglinton Castle Country Park

Published by Mica Publishing
Text and photographs
© **Tom Prentice 2012**

ISBN 978-0-9560367-3-5

Title page: Windy Hill,
Muirshiel Country Park

Maps & design: **Mica Publishing**
www.micapublishing.com

Printed and bound in India by Replika
Press Pvt Ltd

Mica walkers' guides are distributed
by **Cordee Ltd**; info@cordee.co.uk,
www.cordee.co.uk

While every effort has been made to
ensure the accuracy of this guidebook,
paths and access points change over
time. Sturdy footwear and waterproofs are
recommended for all walks, plus a map
and compass for all upland walks.

Approaching Fannyside Loch,
Palacerigg Country Park

Country Parks & Country Estates

Scotland's first Country Park was created in Ayrshire at the National Trust for Scotland's Culzean Castle in 1969. In the following 23 years a further 35 Country Parks were registered, mostly by local authorities, but a number by private estates, or charities such as the National Trust for Scotland (NTS).

The last Country Park was registered in 1992, prior to the replacement of the Countryside Commission for Scotland by Scottish Natural Heritage (SNH) and since then the definition of what is and what is not a Country Park has blurred.

With the need for official registration at an end, estates offering open access and facilities for walkers, such as the privately owned Kelburn Castle at Largs and Drumlanrig Castle north of Dumfries, which might once have registered as Country Parks, now saw no need and titled themselves Country Estates or Country Centres instead.

However, the Country Park title didn't die. Existing Country Parks retained their titles and both local authorities and private estates continued to designate new areas as Country Parks, despite the fact that official registration was no longer required.

Among the newer Country Parks are Cathkin Braes in Glasgow, Plean near Stirling, Roslin Glen and Dalkeith south of Edinburgh and The Hirsel at Coldstream in the Borders. The most recent is Dams to Darnley, a joint project between Glasgow and East Renfrewshire Councils, established in 2008.

So, defining a Country Park is not as simple as it might first appear. Perhaps the best definition of 'Country Parks' in all their guises is offered by SNH which describes them as areas "readily accessible to the public at large, which are actively managed to provide opportunities for people to enjoy the countryside and informal open air recreation.

"All Parks are supported by built facilities and by opportunities to picnic or walk and by programmes of organised events. They are also supported by a Ranger Service to promote visitor enjoyment and understanding of their

• The first Country Park to be registered was Culzean Castle in December 1969. Owned and managed by the National Trust for Scotland, Culzean offers a range of fine walks with extensive sea views

• The most recent Country Park is Dams to Darnley, created by Glasgow and East Renfrewshire Councils in 2008. At its heart lie 'The Dams' which have provided informal recreation for many generations

natural qualities."

Many country houses and estates in Scotland offer access to the public and fall within much of the above definition, but few offer a Scottish Countryside Ranger Service. For the purposes of this guidebook the presence of a **Scottish Countryside Ranger Service**, paid for by the venue, supported by SNH and offering outdoor education and inspiration to young and old, is the defining factor for what is and what is not included.

Regional Parks

Scottish Countryside Rangers are also active in Scotland's three Regional Parks: Clyde Muirshiel above Greenock, the Pentland Hills south of Edinburgh and the Lomond Hills in Fife.

Defined as "large areas of countryside, parts of which are available for informal countryside recreation", these parks all date from the 1980s.

According to SNH the continuing aim of Regional Parks is to "facilitate both the appropriate understanding and enjoyment of the countryside and the integration of this with the other uses of the area, such as farming, forestry and other development, within the context of maintaining and enhancing a quality natural heritage setting".

Between them, the old and new Country Parks and the Regional Parks represent a large part of the rural land owned or managed by Local Authorities.

Scotland's Countryside Parks *Vol 2 – East*

Edinburgh & The Lothians

Polkemmet Country Park
Almondell & Calderwood Country Park
Beecraigs Country Park
Muiravonside Country Park
Hopetoun House Estate
Pentland Hills Regional Park
Bonaly Country Park
Hillend Country Park
Roslin Country Park
Vogrie Country Park
Dalkeith Country Park
Newhailes House Estate NTS
John Muir Country Park

Borders

Bowhill Country Park
The Hirsel Country Park

Fife

Townhill Country Park
Loch Ore Country Park
Lomond Hills Regional Park
Craigtoun Country Park

Angus

Clatto & Camperdown Country Park
Monikie Country Park
Crombie Country Park
Forfar Loch Country Park

Aberdeenshire

Balmedie Country Park
Crathes Castle NTS
Haughton House Country Park
Haddo Country Park NTS
Aden Country Park

Using this Guidebook

Route Maps & Mapping

Route maps accompanying the walks are drawn from out of copyright one inch Ordnance Survey (OS) mapping and half inch Bartholomew mapping, supplemented by in-the-field GPS tracks, and personal observation.

These route maps are only sketch maps and walkers are advised to purchase the up-to-date Ordnance Survey Landranger (1:50,000) or Explorer (1:25,000) scale maps for the walks.

The relevant OS Landranger map for each walk is indicated by 'OS 64' etc in the information panel <www.ordnancesurvey.co.uk>.

Map Symbols

P Car park or layby
P Other parking
▲ Summit
⚐ Golf course

Route Symbols

——— Route on path
······ Route no path
═══ Road
▬▬▬ Route along road
= = = = Track
▪▪▪▪▪ Route along track
- - - - Other path
——— Optional extension

• routes on roads generally follow pavements or verges.

• tracks include all non-tarmac surfaces (farm and forest tracks), and All Terrain Vehicle (ATV) tracks on open hillsides.

• 'pathless' hillsides are often criss-crossed by paths created by sheep, deer, cattle or goats.

Access

The Land Reform (Scotland) Act 2003 grants everyone the right to be on most land and inland water for recreation, providing they act responsibly. These rights and responsibilities are explained in the Scottish Access Code <www.outdooraccess-scotland.com>.

• take personal responsibility for your own actions and act safely;

• respect people's privacy and peace of mind;

• help land managers and others to work safely and effectively;

• care for your environment and take your litter home;

• keep your dog under proper control;

• take extra care if you're organising an event or running a business.

Grades & Times

Most of the routes in this guide follow maintained paths suitable for a variety of abilities. A few, however, take rougher or upland terrain where paths are less obvious. The following grades have been used.

• **Easy**: Low level waymarked routes on mostly level terrain.

• **Easy / Moderate**: Low level waymarked routes, but longer or with inclines or rougher terrain.

• **Moderate**: Higher level routes over hills or moorland, on generally well-marked footpaths.

• **Moderate / Strenuous**: Low and high level routes over some rough terrain. There may be little waymarking and paths may be indistinct in places.

There are no walks graded **Strenuous**

Mugdock Country Park Visitor Centre

in this guide although grading walks is very subjective. For this reason, distance and terrain should also be taken into account when choosing a walk.

Timings are for round trips and include stops for lunch, rest and admiring the view. However, these timings also have a subjective element and the time you take on your walk will be influenced by factors such as fitness, terrain, the nature of the party (large family groups are generally slower than small ones) and the weather.

Equipment & Weather

Stout footwear with a good tread is advisable for all walks. The weather can vary significantly from place to place and from hour to hour, so waterproofs and warm clothing are recommended, especially on hill and moorland walks. Adequate food and water should also be taken, although many of the parks have Visitor Centres with shops and cafes.

Weather forecasting is not easy, but the following websites are worthwhile
<www.metcheck.com>
<www.bbc.co.uk/weather>
BBC tv forecasts can be accessed via terrestrial and satellite services.

Travel

General: Traveline Scotland (0871 2002233) offers a wide range of travel information for national and local bus, rail and ferry services, with links to many websites. <www.travelinescotland.com>
Bus: Stagecoach
<www.stagecoachbus.com>
Rail: Scotrail <www.scotrail.co.uk>

Arran & Ayrshire

Brodick Castle and gardens

*C*astles dominate this chapter, although not all are castles in the true sense of the word. Brodick Castle on the Isle of Arran certainly is, combining a 16th century tower house, parts of which date back to the 14th century, with a Scottish Baronial-Style west wing added in the 19th century. The castle and estate passed to the National Trust for Scotland in 1958.

Brodick's extensive estate and gardens can be combined with tracks in the adjoining forestry to produce three straightforward walks of differing lengths. **Cnocan Gorge [1]** takes a route through the western side of the estate to a deep, pool-filled sandstone gorge, before returning via the graves of the 11th and 12th Dukes of Hamilton. The second route starts up the approach path to Goatfell, Arran's highest mountain, before traversing east through Forestry Commission Scotland land to the wooded **Merkland Burn [2]**. **Dan's Walk [3]** is the shortest of the three and lies on the wooded northern coast of the estate, with fine views across Brodick Bay.

Culzean Castle on the Ayrshire coast was also once a tower house, but was remodelled by Robert Adam in the 18th century to produce one of Scotland's finest country houses. The castle was fortified during the Napoleonic Wars with a small battery of canon, although no shots were fired in anger. Culzean was given to the National Trust for Scotland in 1945. From its cliff-top perch Culzean has

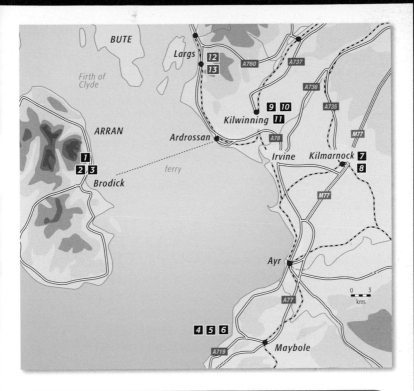

BRODICK CASTLE COUNTRY PARK

Located at Brodick, Isle of Arran

National Trust for Scotland
<www.nts.org.uk>

Getting There

Foot: *From Brodick*

Road: *From Brodick – A841*

Ferry: *Ardrossan-Brodick (car), Claonaig-Lochranza (car)*
<www.calmac.co.uk>

Bus: *See p7*

Facilities

Visitor Centre: *(01770 302202), toilets*

Countryside Ranger Service: *Walks & educational events*

Other Activities: *Adventure playground, Brodick Castle & Gardens*

Food, Drink & Shops: *Castle cafe & restaurant, gifts, arts & crafts, plant sales*

Further Information

Forestry Commission Scotland:

CULZEAN CASTLE COUNTRY PARK

Located at Culzean, south of Ayr

National Trust for Scotland
<www.nts.org.uk>

Getting There
Foot: *From Maidens*

Road: *From Glasgow & Edinburgh – M8, M77, A77, A719. From Stirling – M80, M8, M77, A77, A719*

Bus: *See p7*

Facilities
Visitor Centre: *(0870 1181945), toilets*

Countryside Ranger Service: *Walks & educational events*

Other Activities: *Adventure playground, Culzean Castle & Gardens*

Food, Drink & Shops: *Home Farm shop & restaurant, coffee house, gifts, arts & crafts, books, clothing, plant sales*

DEAN CASTLE COUNTRY PARK

Located at Kilmarnock

East Ayrshire Council
<www.east-ayrshire.gov.uk>

Getting There
Foot: *From Kilmarnock*

Road: *From Glasgow & Edinburgh – M8, M77, A77, B7038. From Stirling – M80, M8, M77, A77, B7038*

Train: *Kilmarnock (1.5km), First ScotRail see p7*

Bus: *See p7*

Facilities
Visitor Centre: *(01563 522702), toilets*

Countryside Ranger Service: *Walks & educational events*

Other Activities: *Adventure playground, Dean Castle museum, pets corner*

Food, Drink & Shops: *Tea room & gift shop*

Further Information
Website: <www.deancastle.com>

EGLINTON CASTLE COUNTRY PARK

Located between Irvine & Kilwinning

North Ayrshire Council
<www.north-ayrshire.gov.uk>

Getting There
Foot: *From Irvine & Kilwinning*

Road: *From Glasgow & Edinburgh – M8, A737, B7038. From Stirling – M80, M8, A73, B7038*

Train: *Kilwinning (3km), Irvine (5km), First ScotRail see p7*

Bus: *See p7*

Facilities
Visitor Centre: *(01294 551776), toilets*

Countryside Ranger Service: *Walks & educational events*

Other Activities: *Adventure playground, bird watching, fishing*

Food, Drink & Shops: *Visitor Centre cafe & gift shop*

Further Information
Forestry Commission Scotland: <www.forestry.gov.uk>

Culzean Castle

magnificent views to the Isle of Arran and offers some high quality walks in the estate and along the coast.

Maidenhead to Culzean [4] culminates in a rough but rewarding adventure round the rocky shore below the castle. Low tide, good weather and suitable footwear are essential. The route along the **Culzean Cliff Tops [5]** is rather easier and gives many opportunities to descend to the coast. The final walk in this park combines the less frequented northern part of the park, location for some recent Stone Age discoveries, with the track bed of **Culzean's Hidden Railway [6]** along the eastern boundary.

Moving inland, Dean Castle dates from the 14th century, but was extensively refurbished from a ruinous condition in the mid-1900s by the 8th and 9th Lord Howard de Walden, before being gifted, along with a collection of arms, armour and historic musical instruments to the people of Kilmarnock in 1975. The park is the smallest in this chapter but contains the confluence of

the Fenwick Water and Crawfurdland Water, both of which are explored in the **Two Waters Walk [7]**. The second walk at Dean Castle follows the resulting river, the Kilmarnock Water, **South to Dean Park [8]**.

Unlike the other castles in this chapter, Eglinton is a ruin. All that remains of this large country house is a facade and one of the four towers. Once home to the Montgomeries, Earls of Eglinton, the house was demolished in the mid-1970s and the estate gifted to the local council. The Country Park opened in 1986 and offers some well-maintained routes **Around the Lochs [9]** and through the surrounding park and agricultural land, with views to the Isle of Arran and the upland of Clyde Muirshiel Regional Park.

Much of the Montgomeries' fortune was built on coal mining, which continued on the estate up to the 1980s. The remains of this industry can still be seen in the last two walks to **Cairnmount Hill [10]** and through **Ladyha' Park [11]**.

Brodick Castle

Brodick Castle and its surrounding woodlands contain an extensive network of trails with many interesting diversions and child-friendly entertainments.

Sections of the tower house date back to the 14th, but most of the castle reflects the 16th century building of the Hamiltons who became Earls of Arran in 1503. The large west wing was added in Scottish Baronial-Style following the marriage of Susan, youngest daughter of wealthy book and art collector William Beckford, to the 10th Duke of Hamilton in 1843. Many of the internal decorations and furnishings came to Brodick from the Beckford collection.

From the National Trust for Scotland (NTS) Visitor Centre ascend towards the terrace which runs between the fine walled garden and the front of the castle. Arran benefits from the warming influence of the Gulf Stream and the formal gardens are worth exploring.

At the far end of the terrace near the entrance to the castle itself, follow a path down and right, signposted Pedestrian Way Out. When it starts to curve down left, turn immediately right on to a much smaller path leading down to the Mill Burn, which features later in the walk.

Cross over the burn then back again and the path emerges back on the main path which descends towards the pedestrian entrance at Cladach. Keep right at the next junction and the next and continue straight ahead to meet the walkers' track up Goatfell, which starts at Cladach. Pass straight over the Goatfell track to the path signposted Easceanoch Trail. Follow this across the

START & FINISH: Brodick Castle NTS car park (NS018381)

DISTANCE: 4.5km; 2.75 miles

TIME: 1hr 30mins

MAP: OS 69; Harvey maps Arran

TERRAIN: Tracks & paths; mostly waymarked, muddy in places

GRADE: Easy

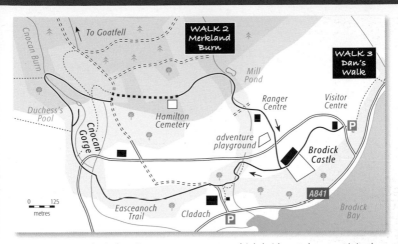

Cnocan Burn and wind up its west bank to cross over the castle access road onto the Cnocan Gorge Trail. This fine sandstone gorge is a reminder that despite the mountain scenery you are still just in the Lowlands. The geological Highland Boundary Fault cuts through the island just to the north of here, splitting Arran into northern Highlands and southern Lowlands.

After a while, a diversion can be made down to the Cnocan Burn to visit the Duchess's Pool, before returning to

cross a high bridge and on to rejoin the wide Goatfell track beyond. Turn left on to the track, ascend a short distance, then turn right onto the Cemetery Trail heading for the Hamilton Family Cemetery. The graveyard is surrounded by a red sandstone wall and railings and contains the headstones of the 11th and 12th Dukes of Hamilton, owners of Brandon and Chatelherault – see walks [38-40] – and the 12th Duke's wife.

From here, continue past the Mill Pond – there isn't much to see but you may hear the lade – and the path descends back towards the castle passing over various bridges, across an access track and through a metal gate to arrive at the Ranger Centre.

If the youngsters with you are still bursting with energy then the adventure playground will help flatten their batteries while you have a cup of tea and take a look round the castle.

Access free – Parking charge

Brodick Castle Country Park (NTS)
Merkland Burn

Beside the Merkland Burn

*I*mmediately north of the fields and parkland surrounding Brodick Castle you enter plantations maintained by Forestry Commission Scotland. A network of tracks and trails crisscross this forestry with names reflecting the area's archaeology and prominent figures from Arran's past.

The elevation of this route offers fine views south over Brodick Bay with the opportunity to explore some hidden corners, and a delightful descent of the Merkland Burn to finish.

As the mature conifers in the plantations are harvested, they are being replaced by Scots pine and deciduous trees such as oak, birch and ash. Many of the tracks are popular with mountain bikers, so keep an ear out for fast moving cyclists.

From the NTS Visitor Centre ascend towards the terrace which runs

between the fine walled garden and the front of the castle. At the far end of the terrace, near the entrance to the castle itself, follow a path down and right, signposted Pedestrian Way Out. When it starts to curve down left, turn immediately right on to a much smaller path leading down to the Mill Burn.

Cross over the burn then back again and the path emerges once more onto the main path, which descends towards the pedestrian entrance at Cladach. Keep right at the next junction and the next and continue straight ahead to meet the walkers' track up Goatfell which starts at Cladach.

Ascend this track with views north-west to Beinn Nuis and cross straight over the access road used by vehicles leaving the castle. Enter into Forestry Commission Scotland woodland, passing the Cnocan Gorge Trail coming

START & FINISH: *Brodick Castle NTS car park (NS018381)*

DISTANCE: *5km; 3 miles*

TIME: *1hr 40mins*

MAP: *OS 69; Harvey maps Arran*

TERRAIN: *Tracks & paths; some waymarks, muddy in places*

GRADE: *Easy*

in from the left and the Cemetery Trail which goes off on the right to the Hamilton Cemetery passed on the **Cnocan Gorge** [1] route.

Slightly higher up at the next junction the Goatfell path and blue-waymarked Balmoral Ride head off to the left. Leave the beaten track at this point by turning right onto the Charcoal Kiln track (the track may not have a name board) and follow this east with fine views over Brodick Bay. Beyond a small bridge over the Mill Burn, the route becomes a footpath which is followed to the first path on the left, signposted Peat Track.

Ascend to join the Balmoral Ride

which comes in from the left. Follow this right and over a ford to reach a bridge over the Merkland Burn. This section of track can be quite muddy from mountain bikes. Just beyond the bridge follow the blue-waymarked path beside the delightful Merkland Burn to rejoin the continuation of the track.

This leads down over the Merkland Burn to just before the main road, where a track leads off right and round to a gate and the start of Lady Mary's Trail. Skirt the fields to exit onto the Brodick Castle access road below the car park.

Access free – Parking charge

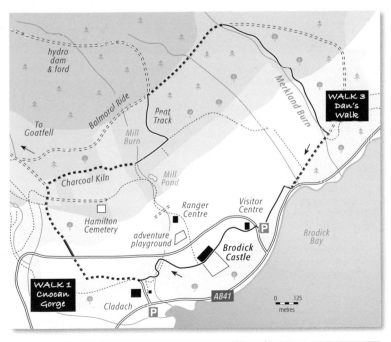

Descending to the granite crag

*n*amed to commemorate the life of Arran naturalist Danny McNicoll, Dan's Walk follows an intricate route through the mixed conifer and broadleaf woodland on the edge of Brodick Bay.

It's a shorter, but a much wilder, experience than other walks in the area, which combines fern-draped trees and crags with unexpected sculptures, to create an adventurous 'lost world' ambience, enhanced by earth paths, numerous junctions and a few sets of log steps along the way.

From Brodick Castle car park follow the access road towards the main road and a blue waymark on the left. This is Lady Mary's Trail, which skirts fields to a gate, from where a track leads round to a larger track just up from the main road. Turn left and ascend this track to a sign on the right indicating Dan's Walk.

Follow this round to a junction, turn right and continue on for a short distance, then go left to a bridge with wooden balustrades over the Merkland Burn. Ascend the steps beyond the bridge and continue to a junction where a path leads off to the right. Follow this past a lattice work sculpture in the wood to arrive at a bridge.

Cross the burn and ascend, keeping left at the next junction then turning

Forest sculpture

START & FINISH: *Brodick Castle NTS car park (NS018381)*

DISTANCE: *3km; 1.75 miles*

TIME: *1hr*

MAP: *OS 69; Harvey maps Arran*

TERRAIN: *Tracks & paths; some waymarks, rough & muddy in places*

GRADE: *Easy / Moderate*

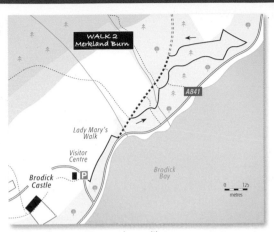

a marker post. From here the path descends a gully beside a large granite crag, skirts round it to the left then ascends to views south to the sea.

Make a steady ascent through old forest via duckboards and rock steps and keep traversing round to a bridge over a burn. Cross this and ascend through a section of high old conifers to exit onto right at the next. Descend steadily on a fairly well–defined level path to a set of log steps. Follow these down then round to the left and over a footbridge and on to another set of wooden steps.

Ascend these and continue round to the track. Turn left and follow the track down and back over the Merkland Burn to connect with the outward route and follow it back to the castle.

Access free – Parking charge

Sea views from Dan's Walk

Culzean from the coast

*C*ulzean's coastline offers a fine low tide outing from Maidenhead Bay to Segganwell, over a wide variety of terrain from sandy beaches to rocky headlands and boulder beaches. The going is scrambly and rough in places, and the boulders sea-washed and slippery, so good footwear and the usual beachcombing care is required. Settled sea and low tide are essential. The coast can be left at a number of points - marked **A** on the map — where it is possible to connect with Culzean's extensive path system.

Exit the Deer Park car park on the lower left side (facing down) to an access road leading left to the Walled Garden with its impressive arched entrance topped by stone urns and flanked by palms. Explore the garden and vinery before exiting at a gate in the south wall (the wall on your left when you entered). Pass through a pergola and continue straight ahead to a junction with the main path (Happy Valley). Follow this to the right, through a tree-lined garden to a four-way path junction. The right turn leads to the Swan Pond and the left direct to a track (Swinston Avenue). Cross straight over, keeping left to exit further down

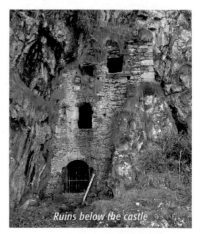
Ruins below the castle

START & FINISH: *Culzean Castle NTS car park (NS232098)*

DISTANCE: *7.5km; 4.5 miles*

TIME: *2hr 50mins*

MAP: *OS 70*

TERRAIN: *Tracks, paths & rocky seashore; rough & slippery in places*

GRADE: *Moderate / Strenuous*

Swinston Avenue.

Continue ahead to pass the Cat Gates, each pillar topped by a stone cat, to the start of a beautiful avenue of trees. Turn right before the avenue onto a track through a short bit of woodland to a grassy track through open land and past a pond to reach a better defined farm access track.

Walk down towards Hogston farm, keeping left at the junction to where the track joins the tarmac road to Maidens. Gain the beach and follow the sand north with fine views over to Ailsa Craig, Arran and Holy Island, with the Mull of Kintyre beyond. Cross the Hodgson Burn where it exits onto the beach below Ardlochan House and continue north towards Barwhin Point.

Traverse the point round to the next sandy beach, Port Carrick, and a path back to the cliff tops. The next headland juts a fair distance into the sea, but it can be avoided if necessary, by a rocky path which leads inland then cuts back down to the shore.

Pass another access point at a laddered boardwalk (leading up to the Powder House), and continue on past the beehive building and Dolphin House Education Centre to a wooden boathouse and sandy bay directly below the castle. From here a path leads up to the West Green Battery.

Continue along the bouldery beach stretching below the

castle cliffs which are mysteriously riddled with caves and ruins, to reach the Gas House with its brick chimney. Beyond this, gain a path rising up on the right and follow it round to the small house of Segganwell, from where concrete steps lead up to a large car park beside Home Farm restaurant and Visitor Centre.

Gain the cliffside path and follow it round above the Gas House to the castle shop and the castle beyond. Go through the white gates round the front of the castle, then drop down to the Fountain Court garden and the West Green Battery beyond. Return to the castle and back through the white gates. Cross the viaduct and through the ruined arch, turning right onto the access road back to the car park.

Access free – Parking charge

WALK 6
Culzean's
Hidden
Railway

Fountain Court garden

*A*rran dominates the western skyline from Culzean's cliff tops, its prominent mountains likened to the facial features of a sleeping giant adrift on the Firth of Clyde. A network of prepared paths hug the tree-fringed cliff edge with panoramic viewpoints and ample opportunity for steep winding descents to hidden sandy beaches; marked with a letter *A* on the walk map.

Leave the Deer Park car park on the lower right side (facing down), following signs to the Castle and Visitor Centre. Turn left through the ruined arch, over the viaduct and left through the white gates to the front of the Castle, then drop down to the Fountain Court garden and West Green Battery.

After exploring the garden and the fine central fountain, descend steps to the lower terrace and turn right towards the sea following signs to West Green Battery, Cliff Walk and the Swan Pond. Pass through a gate in a wall to gain the West Green gun battery from where a path descends to the beach.

The battery of six pounder canon was installed during the Napoleonic Wars and enlarged in later years, although a couple of canon were removed when the summer house was built. The remaining eight, stamped with the name of the manufacturer G.Edington, Glasgow, never fired a shot in anger.

From the end of the battery, signs to the Swan Pond, Cliff Walk and Port Carrick direct you into woodland on an access road. This leads down to Dolphin House Education Centre on the beach, but is soon quit for a path on the left. Beyond this is the Powder House. This turreted building is somewhat hidden in woodland on the right and was built in 1880 to store powder for the battery, the hollow tower being best able to contain an explosion in case of accident. From here another path leads down to the coast.

START & FINISH: *Culzean Castle NTS car park (NS232098)*

DISTANCE: *5.5km; 3.5 miles*

TIME: *1hr 50mins*

MAP: *OS 70*

TERRAIN: *Good tracks & paths, sandy beach; some waymarks*

GRADE: *Easy*

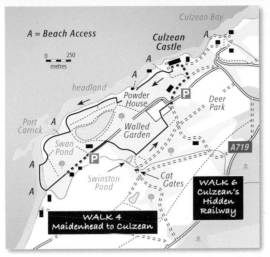

At the next main junction the Cliff Walk is signposted off to the right, while the main path continues straight ahead to the Swan Pond. Turn right and stay on the cliff-top path as it swings round, then make a steep descent to the lowest path. Continue ahead, crossing over the burn draining the Swan Pond, and turn right onto a path.

Pass a path on the right leading down to Port Carrick beach, then skirt round Barwhin Hill with fine open views south and west over sandy Maidenhead Bay to the village of Maidens and Ailsa Craig. A short descent leads to a T-junction, from where a path and boardwalk gain the beach, which is followed towards Maidens to reach the Hogston Burn as it flows out onto the beach below Ardlochan House.

When the tide is in, the burn can be crossed by a footbridge at its mouth and from there a path on its southern side leads back into the woodland to a gate and old cottage. Beyond this a track leads up past Firbank Cottage to the Swan Pond Centre and access road. Just up from the centre turn right onto a path crossing the road heading towards Swinston Pond and the Cat Gates. Follow it past the pond to the second junction on the left opposite a sign to Swan Pond and just after an otter sculpture on the right.

This path is known as Happy Valley and is followed to a point where access left leads to the Walled Garden. After exploring the garden, exit through the impressive urn-topped gateway in the east wall and straight across the access road to the Deer Park car park.

Access free – Parking charge

The Walled Garden

Culzean's Hidden Railway

The Swan Pond

*A*lthough the sleepers and rails have long gone, much of the coastal railway from Ayr to Girvan can still be followed on foot. This includes the southern section from Culzean to Girvan, part of which can be linked with a tour of the castle grounds to make an interesting excursion.

The line crosses the higher ground to the south of the castle and is incut in places. As a result the going can be muddy or wet after rain and appropriate footwear is recommended.

Exit the Deer Park car park on the lower right side (facing down), following signs to the Castle. Turn left through the ruined arch and over the viaduct to the castle, then turn right onto the cliffside path above the Gas House to the Home Farm restaurant, shop and Visitor Centre.

From here follow the 'Way Out' road passing the Events Field and Overflow car park. On the left, just beyond the car park, a path leads into woodland at two small stone gateposts. Follow the path to its end, where it meets the exit road. Turn left up the exit road to a small chapel-like gatehouse from

where a tree-lined track leads through fields, with fine views over to Arran.

In the early 2000s aerial photography of the area revealed ancient settlements and four stone axe heads were subsequently discovered in the field on the right immediately below the caravan site. In 1996 excavation at Kennelmount Cairn, passed later in the walk, had already revealed an early Bronze Age cairn with a perfectly preserved food vessel.

Continue straight on where the track divides at a Culzean boundary sign, then right and round to a gate giving access to the caravan site. Enter this and follow the site access road to the main access road to Culzean Castle. Follow this leftwards past the entry pay kiosk, then left and left again to reach Kennelmount Picnic area with parking, viewpoint and information about the cairn. Continue straight ahead on a track, then drop down to the old railway. Follow this across two bridges to a third bridge which passes over the line, from where steps lead up on the right to a track.

START & FINISH: *Culzean Castle NTS car park (NS232098)*

DISTANCE: *8km; 5 miles*

TIME: *2hrs 40mins*

MAP: *OS 70*

TERRAIN: *Tracks & paths; some waymarks, muddy in places*

GRADE: *Easy / Moderate*

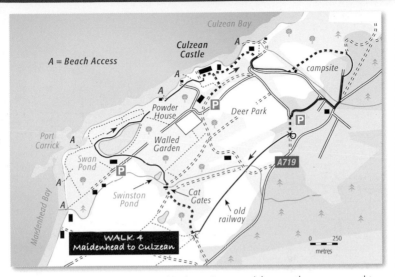

A = Beach Access

Culzean Bay

Culzean Castle

campsite

Powder House

Deer Park

Port Carrick

Walled Garden

Swan Pond

Maidenhead Bay

Swinston Pond

Cat Gates

old railway

A719

0   250
metres

**WALK 4
Maidenhead to Culzean**

Turn right and descend the tree-lined avenue to the Cat Gates where the track swings right (Swinston Avenue). Leave the track by continuing straight ahead and left on a path and follow this to a junction where a left turn is made to the Swan Pond.

Cat Gates

Cross straight over the access road to the western end of the Swan Pond and past the Swan Pond Centre and the boathouse to the far side. Remain on the main path round the pond then straight ahead and right passing the Powder House, from where a path can be taken down to the coast.

Exit onto an access road (a left leads to Dolphin House Education Centre) and follow it up right to the summer house and West Green Battery on the left. Walk past the canons (the path on the left gives access to the coast) and go right through a gate in the wall to the Fountain Court garden.

After exploring this, ascend steps to the terraces and the front of the castle. Go left through the white gates, right over the viaduct and through the arch - way, then right again to the car park.

Access free – Parking charge

25

Dean Castle

Powerbase of the influential Boyd family for more than 400 years, Dean Castle's substantial three storey defensive tower dates from the mid-1300s, built on land granted by Robert Bruce.

Successive generations extended Dean Castle, but by 1745 it was all over. An extensive fire seriously damaged the castle in 1735 and the lands were forfeited to the Crown on the execution of the 4th Earl, William Boyd, following the '45. For the next 150 years it lay in ruins.

The buildings were restored by Thomas Evelyn Ellis, 8th Lord Howard de Walden during the first half of the 20th century and housed his collections of medieval German and Italian armour and early musical instruments. The castle, collections and surrounding parkland were gifted to the people of Kilmarnock by the 9th Lord in 1975.

From the main car park follow the signs for the Visitor Centre to gain the Woodland Trail ascending from its right-hand side. At the five-way junction continue ahead and right following yellow waymarks to the graves of the 8th Lord, his wife Margherita van Raalte and his mother Blanche.

Go over the next junction and on to another where a left turn is taken

START & FINISH: *Dean Castle car park (NS435392)*

DISTANCE: *3.5km; 2 miles*

TIME: *1hr 10mins*

MAP: *OS 70*

TERRAIN: *Waymarked tracks & paths*

GRADE: *Easy*

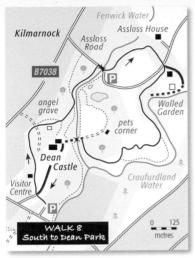

Fenwick Water

Kilmarnock

Assloss House

Assloss Road

B7038

angel grave

P

Walled Garden

pets corner

Dean Castle

Visitor Centre

Craufurdland Water

P

0   125
metres

WALK 8
South to Dean Park

followed soon after by a right where the path divides. Descend via a wooden balustrade following red and blue waymarks to the Fenwick Water and continue beside this to Assloss Road. Follow the road down right and over the bridge, then turn left onto the upper of

two paths with a red waymark.

Ascend to fields and Dean Castle Riding Centre to meet Assloss Road, opposite a track on the left and a red waymarked path on the right. The track leads down to the old walled garden and a ford over the Craufurdland Water (the bridge shown on some park maps is long gone), so a return has to be made to Assloss Road.

The red route passes through fine woodland, with views down to the river and the walled garden, then descends to fields containing livestock before dividing. One path passes through the fields, the other sticks to the riverside, before they join again. Continue beside the river to the bridge over the Fenwick Water at the back of the Castle. Cross over and round to the front of the Castle and the entrance into the courtyard between the Tower House and the modern house – the Dower House. Having admired the armour on display follow the main access drive back to the car park.

Access & Parking free

Above the Fenwick Water

Fenwick Water

Despite its close proximity to Kilmarnock and the busy A77, the deep-cut burns of the Fenwick Water and Craufurdland Water and the surrounding woodland cut out much of the urban noise. This tranquillity is a far cry from the 1800s when a massive sandstone quarry and tile factory occupied the fields of the Rare Breeds Centre, supplying the building materials for a fast-expanding Kilmarnock. Production stopped in 1872 and the quarry was later flooded as a possible reservoir. This was never used and the site was in-filled and landscaped in 1950.

From the main car park follow the signs for the Visitor Centre to gain the Woodland Trail ascending from its right-hand side. At the five-way junction continue ahead and right following yellow waymarks to the graves of the 8th Lord, his wife Margherita van Raalte and his mother Blanche. Go over the next junction and on to another where a left is taken and followed through further woodland to exit onto Assloss Road.

Turn right and down to the bridge, then right again onto a tarmac cycle path alongside the river. This leads south past a wildlife pond to a junction on the left with the Woodland Trail, which is followed round past a large pond to the pets corner. Continue on past the adventure playground to a bridge over the Fenwick Water at the back of the Castle. Cross over and round to the front of the Castle and the entrance into the courtyard between the Tower House and the modern house – the Dower House.

After admiring the armour on display in the Tower House return to the bridge and follow the tarmac cycle route beside the river to the

START & FINISH: *Dean Castle car park (NS435392)*

DISTANCE: *3.5km; 2 miles*

TIME: *1hr 10mins*

MAP: *OS 70*

TERRAIN: *Tracks & paths; some waymarking*

GRADE: *Easy*

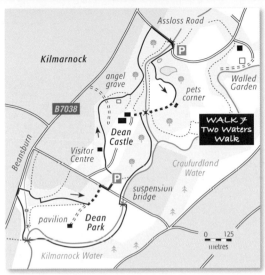

cycle path leading to another footbridge. Cross back over the river, turn right before the steps and walk alongside a wall to a small footbridge into Dean Park. Don't cross this but continue to the main road – Beansburn.

Turn right and follow Beansburn for a short way. Take the first right to re-enter the park, then right again at the junction to gain a high path which is followed round to steps. Descend these to a lower path through woodland, then down

confluence of the Fenwick Water and Craufurdland Water. Continue past the car park to exit at the ford on Dean Road.

Cross the road and over the suspension bridge to the south bank of what is now the Kilmarnock Water and a

to join the lowest path at the access road to the pavilion, which is followed back to Dean Road and the Dean Castle car park.

Access & Parking free

Kilmarnock Water

Eglinton Castle ruins

*E*glinton Castle was built for Hugh Montgomerie, 12th Earl of Eglinton, in 1802, on the back of political power, Ayrshire coal mining and the industrial revolution. Today, little is left standing save for one tall tower, part of the frontage and the foundations. The castle is most associated with Archibold, 13th Earl and Hugh's grandson, who hosted a flamboyant three day medieval-style tournament in the castle grounds in 1839, attracting 80,000 visitors, despite inclement weather.

With the tournament and a passion for breeding and racing horses, Archibold burned a substantial hole in the family fortune, using his vast income from coal mining combined with the sale of many of the family's estates in central Scotland including the port of Ardrossan which his grandfather had helped to fund, to maintain his extravagant lifestyle. The family's fortunes took another blow with the collapse of the Glasgow Bank in 1878. Steady deterioration of the mansion house led to de-roofing in the 1920s and wartime use of the estate for training hastened the deterioration.

In 1950 it was sold to Clement Wilson who established a canning factory. Over the next 20 years, Wilson ploughed substantial sums into the estate, planting trees and refurbishing the stables and many smaller buildings. The house however, could not be saved and was demolished in 1973, leaving part of the outer wall and one of the towers. Wilson gifted the estate to the local council in 1976.

The Country Park opened in 1986 and offers a network of well-maintained

START & FINISH: *Eglinton Castle car park (NS320419)*

DISTANCE: *5km; 3 miles*

TIME: *1hr 40mins*

MAP: *OS 70*

TERRAIN: *Waymarked tracks & paths; muddy in places*

GRADE: *Easy*

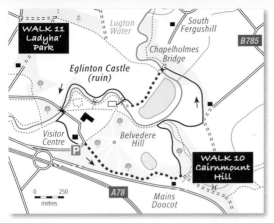

and mostly waymarked paths through the park, wood and farmland on either side of the Lugton Water which runs through the estate.

From the main car park by the Visitor Centre and Tournament Cafe go past the coach park, from where a path goes straight ahead then splits almost immediately. Go right on a tarmac path through woodland to the blonde sandstone Mains Doocot, all that remains after Eglinton Mains farm was demolished to make way for the new road.

Continue round left to a junction and turn left through conifer woodland then open ground with views across to Eglinton Castle tower with hills and wind turbines beyond, to reach a path by the Lugton Water, signposted New Town Trail.

Turn right and follow this path to a four-way junction. Go left here and on to another junction before the black-railinged Chapelholms Bridge, where a track veers off right to South Fergushill. Turn left over the bridge on a continuation of the track towards the castle

ruins, passing Eglinton Loch to arrive at Castle Bridge over the Lugton Water which gives access to the castle ruins. Cross back over Castle Bridge, then left beside the river to the newly restored Tournament Bridge. Continue on beside the river to a stone bridge and access road. Cross over the bridge and turn right, keeping left at the junction on a path back to the car park and Visitor Centre.

Access & Parking free

Eglinton's remaining tower

Eglinton Castle Country Park
Cairnmount Hill

Cairnmount Hill

ive large upright boulders stand on the summit of Cairnmount Hill in the eastern section of the park. While they look suitably ancient, they actually date from the late 1980s when the area was reclaimed and landscaped following closure of the Sourlie open-cast coal mine which occupied the site.

Since the 1700s coal mines had been sunk all over the Eglinton Estate, generating the wealth that made the 12th Earl's mansion and the 13th Earl's extravagance possible; and the associated bings and industrial debris can still be found. The Sourlie mine opened in 1983 and was both the last to open and the last to close.

From the main car park by the Visitor Centre and Tournament Cafe go past the coach park, from where a path goes straight ahead then splits almost immediately. Go right on a tarmac path through woodland to the blonde sandstone Eglinton Mains Doocot.

Continue round to the left, remaining on the main path and ignoring various turnings off to the left, to pass a bridge with black railings and exit into open country. Straight ahead the small hill is topped with an impressive collection of five upright stones and makes a fine viewpoint over the surrounding landscape to the hills and wind turbines above West Kilbride.

Descend the other side to enter the Scottish Wildlife Trust reserve of Sourlie Wood and turn left at the junction. Woodland soon gives way to open ground and a footbridge over the Draught Burn, from where a steady ascent leads past various left turnings to a four-way junction.

Continue straight ahead to meet the Lugton Water and follow it to Chapelholms Bridge, where a track veers off right to South Fergushill. Turn left over the bridge on a continuation

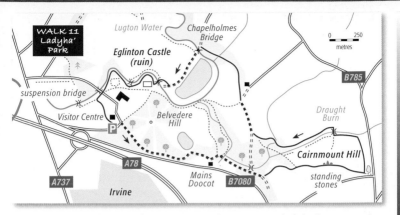

START & FINISH: *Eglinton Castle car park (NS320419)*

DISTANCE: *7.5km; 4.5 miles*

TIME: *2hrs 30mins*

MAP: *OS 70*

TERRAIN: *Waymarked tracks & paths*

GRADE: *Easy*

of the track towards the castle ruins, passing Eglinton Loch to arrive at Castle Bridge over the Lugton Water. Cross over to the castle ruins. After exploring the ruins walk back towards the bridge and go left to follow the red-waymarked riverside path round through woodland to the recently restored Tournament Bridge. Continue beside the river and past the formal gardens to an access road with a stone bridge on the right. Cross straight over the access road keeping left at the junction and follow the path back to the car park.

Access & Parking free

Isle of Arran from Cairnmount Hill

The folly on Belvedere Hill

This route ventures to some of the less-frequented corners of the country park combining waymarked and non-waymarked paths.

From the main car park by the Visitor Centre and Tournament Cafe go past the coach park, from where a path goes straight ahead then splits almost immediately. Turn left through a green gate and on a short way, then right following a Woodland Walk sign to ascend Belvedere Hill to the folly and views west to Arran.

Head over right to a horse gate and kissing gate, descend back to the tarmac path and follow it left to the blonde sandstone doocot of Eglinton Mains. Keep left here and continue round past a left turning, to a second turning beside a burn.

Follow the woodland path beside the burn, muddy in places, to the re-constructed Ice House up on the left. Reputedly built for the 10th Earl, it would have housed ice for the mansion long before the invention of household refrigerators.

Continue over the footbridge to join the gravel path beside the Lugton Water and turn left towards the tower of Eglinton Castle which can be seen protruding above the distant trees.

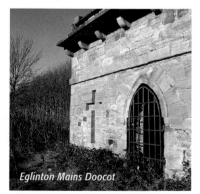

Eglinton Mains Doocot

START & FINISH: *Eglinton Castle car park (NS320419)*

DISTANCE: *6.5km; 4 miles*

TIME: *2hrs 10mins*

MAP: *OS 70*

TERRAIN: *Tracks & paths; some waymarks, rough & muddy in places*

GRADE: *Easy / Moderate*

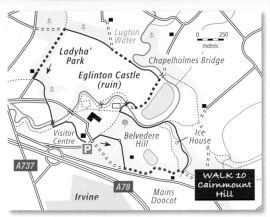

Ladyha' Park

Lugton Water

Chapelholmes Bridge

Eglinton Castle (ruin)

Visitor Centre

P

Belvedere Hill

Ice House

A737

A78

Irvine

Mains Doocot

0   250
metres

WALK 10 Cairnmount Hill

After exploring the ruins cross the nearby Castle Bridge back over the Lugton Water and on past the loch towards the black-railinged Chapelholms Bridge.

Just before the bridge cross the wire fence on the left by the old metal gate and follow the path between the field and the Lugton Water below. The path becomes a grassy track through farmland with fields on both sides and views left to the castle tower. Pass through the first set of gates – this area can be very muddy – but veer right before the second set to an old wooden gate at the corner of the woodland.

From here a good path leads beside fields to a four-way junction. Turn left and follow the track down past a house to arrive at its access road. Turn left here and through horse gates into woodland, passing the ruins of the 568 foot deep Ladyha No2 colliery which closed in 1934, to arrive at an access road. Here there are two choices. Either cross over and straight ahead to the suspension bridge, or cross over and turn right onto a field-edge path which can be followed round to the suspension bridge.

Cross over the bridge, built by the Royal Engineers in 1987, then left towards the access road. A right at the next junction just before the road leads back to the Visitor Centre and car park.

Access & Parking free

Eglinton Castle tower from the park

Muirshiel & Inverclyde

Finlaystone house

lyde Muirshiel Regional Park
covers most of the high
ground south of Greenock
and dominates this chapter. Much
of the Park is open, heather-covered
moorland containing many reservoirs,
and dotted with sheep farms. The
steeper flanks of this upland area offer
wider diversity as burns tumble through
narrow wooded glens to the arable
land surrounding the Clyde coast.

On the southern fringes of the
Regional Park, the wooded **Kelburn
Glen** [12] at Kelburn Castle offers the
very best example of this landscape: a
beautiful gorge with pools and waterfalls, accessed by a well-maintained

path network. The more extensive
Countess Walk [13] provides the
opportunity to explore the formal
gardens of the 16th century home of
the Earls of Glasgow, followed by a
wider traverse of the estate with extensive views over the Firth of Clyde.

At Largs just to the north,
Auchenmaid & Gogo Glen [14] gives a
pleasant ramble into the high moorland
below Irish Law, while **Knock Hill** [15]
offers a slightly more challenging walk
to a prominent isolated summit with
extensive views over the town.

The next five walks are easily
accessed from the Greenock Cut Visitor
Centre by Loch Thom to the north. The

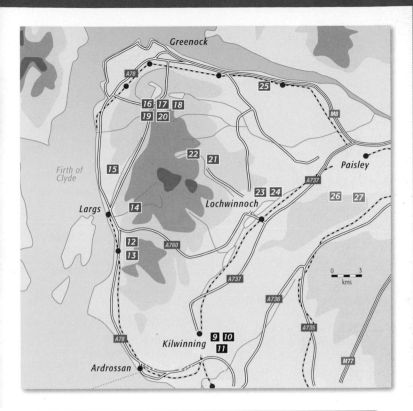

KELBURN CASTLE COUNTRY CENTRE

Located south of Largs

Kelburn Castle
<www.kelburnestate.com>

Getting There
Foot: *From Largs*

Road: *From Glasgow & Edinburgh – M8, A737, A760, A78. From Stirling – M80, M8, A737, A760, A78*

Train: *Largs (3km), First ScotRail see p7*

Bus: *See p7*

Facilities
Visitor Centre: *(01475 568685), toilets*

Countryside Ranger Service: *Walks & educational events*

Other Activities: *Adventure Course, Secret Forest, playbarn, museum*

Food, Drink & Shops: *Cafe & shop, gifts, arts & crafts*

CLYDE MUIRSHIEL REGIONAL PARK

Occupies the high ground between Greenock, West Kilbride and Lochwinnoch

Clyde Muirshiel Regional Park
<www.clydemuirshiel.co.uk>

Renfrewshire Council
<www.renfrewshire.gov.uk

Inverclyde Council
<www.inverclyde.gov.uk>

North Ayrshire Council
<www.north-ayrshire.gov.uk>

Getting There

Foot: From Greenock, Largs, Lochwinnoch and local villages

Road: From Glasgow & Edinburgh – M8, A78, minor roads. From Stirling – M80, M8, A78, minor roads

Train: Greenock West (2km), Drumfrochar-Greenock (900m), Largs (1km). First ScotRail see p7

Bus: See p7

Facilities

Greenock Cut Visitor Centre: (01475 521458), toilets

Countryside Ranger Service: Walks & educational events

Other Activities: Greenock Cut exhibition, wildlife cameras

Food & Drink: Cafe & gift shop

MUIRSHIEL COUNTRY PARK

Located north-west of Lochwinnoch

Clyde Muirshiel Regional Park
<www.clydemuirshiel.co.uk>

Renfrewshire Council
<www.renfrewshire.gov.uk

Getting There

Road: From Glasgow & Edinburgh – M8, A737, A760, B786, minor roads. From Stirling – M80, M8, A737, A760, B786, minor roads

Train & Bus: No practical services (Lochwinnoch station 10km)

Facilities

Visitor Centre: (01505 842803), toilets

Countryside Ranger Service: Walks & educational events

Other Activities: Wildlife cameras

Food & Drink: Cafe & gift shop

FINLAYSTONE COUNTRY ESTATE

Located east of Port Glasgow

Finlaystone Estate
<www.finlaystone.co.uk>

Getting There

Foot: From Port Glasgow

Road: From Glasgow & Edinburgh – M8, A8. From Stirling – M80, M8, A8

Train: Langbank (1.5km), Woodhall-Port Glasgow (2km). First ScotRail see p7

Bus: See p7

Facilities

Visitor Centre: (01475 540505), toilets

Countryside Ranger Service: Walks & educational events

Other Activities: Adventure playground, estate gardens, doll museum

Food, Drink & Shops: Tearoom & cafe, gift shop, plant sales, toys, books

Greenock Cut [19] aqueduct is well known and supplied water to Greenock's industry and people for more than 170 years, but the lesser known Kelly Cut [16] and 'Wee' Cut [20] offer interesting and slightly wilder walks. Two other walks can be made from the Visitor Centre. Shielhill Nature Trail [17] explores the delightful rocky and wooded glen of the Kip Water, while Hillside Hill & Dunrod Hill [18] traverses the small tops immediately to the north. All of the high ground accessible from the Visitor Centre is open and exposed with little shelter. This presents fine views, but also means adequate warm and waterproof clothing is recommended for these walks.

Access to the eastern part of the Regional Park is via Muirshiel Country Park. Windy Hill [21] is an excellent introductory hillwalk for youngsters with waymarks, boardwalks and a panoramic view, while the route out to the deserted Muirshiel Barytes Mine [22] penetrates deep into the wind-swept moorland via the old access track.

Castle Semple Country Park lies in the south-eastern section of the Regional Park. Castle Semple Loch provides the focus for this park and two fine routes. The first visits Parkhill Wood [23] and 16th century Castle Semple Collegiate Church, while the second traverses open agricultural land surrounding Kenmure Temple [24], once a deer-viewing tower on the historic Castle Semple estate. Both routes make use of the cycle track on the disused railway through the village.

The final walk in this chapter lies immediately north, at Finlaystone Estate [25] on the south bank of the River Clyde. The described route encompasses the estate's extensive broadleaf woodland and the formal gardens of the mansion-house, utilising the network of waymarked paths.

CASTLE SEMPLE COUNTRY PARK

Located at Lochwinnoch

Clyde Muirshiel Regional Park
<www.clydemuirshiel.co.uk>

Renfrewshire Council
<www.renfrewshire.gov.uk

Getting There
Foot: From Lochwinnoch

Road: From Glasgow & Edinburgh – M8, A737, A760. From Stirling – M80, M8, A737, A760

Train: Lochwinnoch (1.5km). First ScotRail see p7

Bus: See p7

Facilities
Visitor Centre: (01505 842882), toilets

Countryside Ranger Service: Walks & educational events

Other Activities: Wide range of water sports instruction & courses, boat hire, mountain bike hire, sustrans cycle route, fishing, bird hides – RSPB Lochwinnoch

Food, Drink & Shops: Visitor Centre cafe & gift shop

Further Information
Parkhill Wood website:
<www.discoverclydemuirshiel.co.uk/parkhill/>

RSPB Lochwinnoch:

Kelburn Glen

Brazilian graffiti at Kelburn Castle

Muirshiel Regional Park's western edge meets the Firth of Clyde in a swift transition from hilly heather-clad moorland to arable farmland. This narrow, fertile strip is fringed with woodland and scoured by deep, narrow glens from the heavy upland rainfall on its short, swift journey to the sea.

The finest and most accessible of these is Kelburn Glen in the grounds of Kelburn Castle and Country Centre. Here, the Kel Burn draining from the ubiquitous upland reservoirs of Muirhead and Camphill, descends in a series of gorges separated by pools and waterfalls.

This magical place can be appreciated by walkers of all ages and abilities, thanks to an extensive network of paths and bridges, overlooked by Kelburn Castle. Home to the Boyle family, Earls of Glasgow, the tower

house dates from the 16th century, the mansion-house from the 18th.

In 2007, following a conservation report stating the tower house's concrete facing needed replacement, the 10th Earl offered the outside walls as a massive temporary canvas to four leading graffiti artists from Brazil. The result was both startling and unique.

The North Glen Path is slightly steeper in ascent, but descending the South Glen Path offers the best views of the castle and the Clyde islands.

From the car park walk towards the Visitor Centre, then up between the cafe and shop. Turn left by the 'stockade' and pass below the green-fronted museum to a four-way junction. The route continues down steps to Sanham's Bridge, but first a detour should be made up right then down left to the Waterfall Pool. Sea trout have been found here, prevented from

START & FINISH: *Kelburn Castle car park (NS216565)*

DISTANCE: *3km; 1.75 miles*

TIME: *1hr*

MAP: *OS 63*

TERRAIN: *Waymarked tracks & paths; steep in places*

GRADE: *Easy / Moderate*

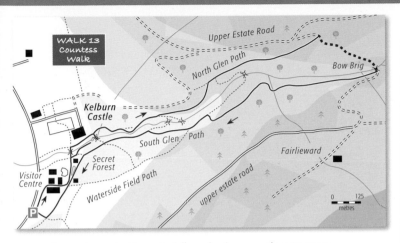

progressing upstream by the waterfall.

Return to the bridge and cross over. Originally called Jubilee Bridge in commemoration of Queen Victoria's Silver Jubilee, the monarch's celebration was superseded by that of Frank Sanham, butler to the 8th and 9th Earls, who crossed it several times a day for more than 30 years.

Ahead, the walled Plaisance Garden is well worth a visit, before returning to the path below the tower and following it up the north side of the glen past the Ice House to a junction signposted right to Kelburn Bridge and left to North Glen Path and Monument. Turn right to visit Kelburn Bridge above the Waterfall Pool, before returning to the North Glen Path.

Keep right to visit the Monument, from where signposts to North Glen and Upper Glen are followed on a zigzag path up through the glen to a more level path and the Upper Estate Road access track. Turn right, signposted South Glen Path, and follow the track across the stone Bow Brig over the upper Kel Burn. Shortly after this turn right onto the South Glen Path and follow this down, keeping left at the first junction and right at the second, back to the start.

The Waterfall Pool

Access & Parking charge

41

Firth of Clyde from the viewpoint

anoramic views across the Firth of Clyde are the main feature of this walk which makes a wide tour of Kelburn Castle estate utilising the Countess Walk and the Upper Estate Road.

From the car park walk towards the Visitor Centre, then up beside the cafe and shop. Turn left by the 'stockade' and pass below the green-fronted museum to a four-way junction. The route continues down steps and over Sanham's Bridge, then ascends to Kelburn Castle and straight ahead through a gate into the walled Plaisance Garden.

After exploring the garden exit at a gate on the far side onto the castle access road and cross straight ahead to a grassy path beside a fence enclosing the New Zealand Garden. The 7th Earl was Governor from 1892 to 1897 and returned with trees and shrubs which have thrived in the warm and moist Firth of Clyde climate.

Turn right at the track and ascend it,

keeping an eye out for a pedestrian gate on the left which gives access to the Countess Walk; a wide grassy ride between fenced fields.

Follow the ride up through two gates with expansive views across fields to the coast, marina and Great Cumbrae island. Where the ride ends go right over a footbridge then over two more and on to join the Upper Estate Road.

Turn right, left is signposted to Largs and ascend past the so-called Corkscrew Road coming in from the right, to meet a second junction. Here one branch of the track continues climbing on the left, the other curves off to the right on a

START & FINISH: *Kelburn Castle car park (NS216565)*

DISTANCE: *5km; 3 miles*

TIME: *1hr 40mins*

MAP: *OS 63*

TERRAIN: *Waymarked tracks & paths; rough in places*

GRADE: *Easy / Moderate*

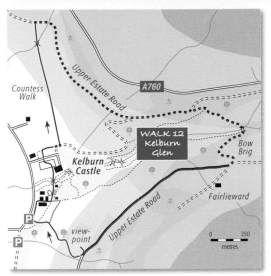

Countess Walk

Upper Estate Road

A760

WALK 12
Kelburn
Glen

Bow Brig

Kelburn Castle

view-point

Upper Estate Road

Fairlieward

P

P

0   250
metres

Glen Path which heads off just after the bridge and zigzag up to a junction with a path coming in from the left signposted Haylie Brae and Gogoside. Keep right to gain the tarmac access track to Fairlieward and follow it down to a viewpoint with a stylised indicator map and benches.

From here a new gravel path winds down between fields to woodland from where an obvious path continues down through trees and rhododendrons to the

more level route. Follow the right-hand track round to where it is joined by the North Glen Path ascending from Kelburn Glen and cross over Bow Brig.

Stick on the track passing the South

car park. Alternatively turn right below fields to the Countryside Ranger Office, cafe and shop.

Access & Parking charge

Kelburn woodland

Picnic by the Greeto Water

*A*uchenmaid Craigs is a small hillock easily reached from Largs via the track above the Gogo Water and offers a pleasant and relatively straightforward route with fine views over the town and the Firth of Clyde. The hill can be climbed from various directions with a return alongside the Gogo Water if desired.

Start from a small parking area at the top of Bellesdale Avenue beyond Largs Academy. Walk back down the road for a short distance, then right and through a gate onto a tarmac access road leading to phone masts.

Beyond these, continue on a track through another gate and on to a third with a stile and a wall. The first route up Auchenmaid Craigs starts here and follows the right side of the wall to a grassy and often marshy track leading to stone sheep pens.

The grassy track now leads uphill left of the crags to meet a wall at a gate, from where it continues, again marshy in

places, until the summit aerials come into view. From the top, Knock Hill, Irish Law and Kaim Hill are the principal hills to the north, east and south while the view west is dominated by the hills of Cowal, Arran, Bute and Kintyre.

From the abandoned and rusting aerial follow the grassy track to a green

START & FINISH: Bellesdale Avenue, Largs (NS212593)

DISTANCE: 5.5km; 3.5 miles

TIME: 1hr 50mins

MAP: OS 63

TERRAIN: Tracks & paths; boggy in places

GRADE: Moderate

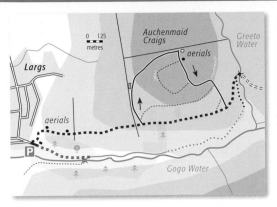

descending the Greeto Water for a short distance below the bridge to view a fine waterfall and pool. From here return to the track and follow it back to Largs with some fine views over to Arran.

Alternatively, a rougher and more adventurous path can be followed beside the Gogo Water. For this, continue descending

aerial and continue to gain a grassy track descending the hillside directly south into the Gogo Glen. Near the main track this descent route divides, but both paths lead to the track below.

This route could also be used for ascent and descent offering a shorter and drier, if steeper and slightly less interesting, alternative. A green waymark indicates the start of the route from the main track.

Once back at the main track continue up the glen to Greeto Bridge where there is a nice flat spot for a picnic. Before returning to Largs, it is worth

to the Gogo Water and follow it to woodland. Enter this just above the river to gain a path. A rocky area needs to be negotiated followed by a marshy section, but once clear of these the route is relatively dry, although tiring in places with exposed tree roots and rocks. The best route stays close to the river bank, eventually becoming a track leading to a footbridge over the Gogo Water. Don't cross over but ascend the track on the right back to Bellesdale Avenue.

Access & Parking free

Above the Gogo Water

Clyde Muirshiel Regional Park
Knock Hill

Brisbane Mains

Knock Hill, or The Knock as it is named on Ordnance Survey maps, isn't very high but it offers a fantastic view over the Clyde islands to Cowal and Kintyre.

With a view like that it's not surprising that the hill is topped with the remains of an Iron Age fort. Unfortunately, this has been flattened in places by a spiral track up which ladies are reputed to have been conveyed for picnics, while their husbands enjoyed the shooting on Lord Kelvin's Nether Hall estate below.

Archaeological destruction aside, this same track offers the walker a straight-forward, if sometimes rather marshy, means of access to this high vantage point. The ladies and their carriage have long departed, but Knock Hill remains an excellent location for a picnic on a fine day.

The walk starts from Aubery Crescent at the north end of Largs seafront, easily reached from the train station or the main car park at Largs pier. From Aubery Crescent follow the coastal path round the playpark and pond and beside Noddsdale Water to the main road. Follow this right a short way and cross over with care to Barr Crescent (signposted Ayrshire Coastal Paths Skermorlie). Continue up this and Noddleburn Road beyond, then left onto a tarmac path between the burn and houses, when the road swings right.

When the path rejoins the road higher up, turn left to meet Brisbane Glen Road and follow that leftwards, again signposted Ayrshire Coastal Path. The pavement ends near the cemetery and a cairn on the left marking the life of Sir Thomas MacDougall Brisbane, amateur astronomer and Governor General of New South Wales, who gave his name to the Australian city of Brisbane.

START & FINISH: *Aubery Crescent, Largs (NS199603)*

DISTANCE: *11.5km; 7 miles*

TIME: *3hrs 50mins*

MAP: *OS 63*

TERRAIN: *Tracks & paths; boggy in places*

GRADE: *Moderate / Strenuous*

regains the track which divides shortly after at the top of a small wooded glen. The left-hand signposted track leads up and out onto more open hillside and views north to the high hills of Cowal and Arrochar. Turn left at the next junction and follow the track to below Knock Hill from where a direct ascent can be made, or a more leisurely spiral ascent via the ladies' track.

From the summit return to the main junction and turn left, following the track and fields down beside the woodland on the edge of the Blackhouse Burn to gain the road at the bottom, which leads left back to Largs. However, if the golf course below is quiet then it is possible to descend the south ridge to a fence and wall and cross the course (over which walkers have a legal right of access providing they do not interfere with golfer's recreation), to join the minor road.

This road emerges on the main road by the Nether Hall gatehouse, where a blue plaque marks William Thomson Lord Kelvin of Largs, best known for his 'degrees K' absolute temperature scale, used, among other things, in digital cameras for determining white balance.

Continue up the road with views left to the farmhouse of Brisbane Mains and Knock Hill to gain the farmhouse track, signposted to the High Road and Knock Hill. A gate at the back of the farm gives access to a rougher and steeper track which gives increasingly good views to the surrounding hills and south over Largs.

A short diversion round a sheep pen

Access & Parking free

Knock Hill summit

Moorland track leading to Knock Hill

East Hill from the Kelly Cut

*I*n the early 19th century, in response to demands for water from Greenock's expanding population and industry, a network of reservoirs and aqueducts was developed on the high ground above the city by civil engineer Robert Thom.

Nearly 200 years later the paths and tracks created to service this water supply offer excellent walking. Not that recreation on this high moorland is something new. In his poem *Loch Thom*, W.S.Graham recalls boyhood walks 'up from Greenock' in the early 1920s: the loch, the distant firth and blue moors of Ayrshire, and the haunting cry of the curlew.

Of the two aqueducts, the Kelly Cut transports water across Leap Moor from Kelly Reservoir to Loch Thom, acting as a feeder for the much better known **Greenock Cut** [19]. Kelly Cut isn't such an impressive work of engineering as its twin and isn't a

Daff Reservoir

scheduled monument either. Alas, sections of the aqueduct wall are in a poor state of repair as a consequence.

Greenock Cut Visitor Centre (previously named Cornalees Bridge) lies at the southern end of the Loch Thom compensation reservoir below **Hillside Hill & Dunrod Hill [18]** and offers the best starting point for all the walks in the area.

From the car park follow the road back towards Cornalees Bridge and cross over this and the modern bridge

START & FINISH: *Greenock Cut
Visitor Centre car park (NS247722)*
DISTANCE: *12km; 7.5 miles*
TIME: *4hrs*

MAP: *OS 63*

TERRAIN: *Tracks & paths; muddy
in places*

GRADE: *Moderate*

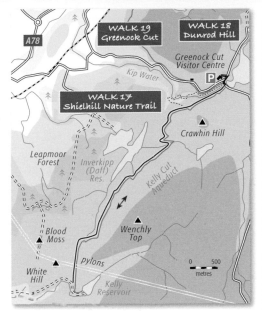

WALK 19
Greenock Cut

WALK 18
Dunrod Hill

Greenock Cut
Visitor Centre

Kip Water

WALK 17
Shielhill Nature Trail

Crawhin Hill

Leapmoor
Forest

Inverkipp
(Daff)
Res.

Kelly Cut
Aqueduct

Blood
Moss

Wenchly
Top

pylons

White
Hill

Kelly
Reservoir

0   500
metres

A78

After a short distance
Shielhill Nature Trail [17]
joins the cut path via a
boardwalk ascending the
moorland on the right.
Further on, Inverkipp
(Daff) Reservoir marks
the half-way point in the
walk, the high mountains
of Arrochar and Cowal on
the other side of the Firth
of Clyde providing an
impressive backdrop. It's
a fairly bleak spot domi-
nated by moorland,
tussocky grass and scat-
tered sheep – not
somewhere to be caught
in a downpour.

At the Kelly Reservoir
the path becomes an
access track and starts a
long descent beside the
Kelly Burn to Weymss
Bay. This provides a good

beyond, to a gate on the right indicating the start of the Kelly Cut. The
route is level and obvious, although a
little rough and muddy in places, so
adequate footwear is recommended.

point at which to turn round and
reverse the outward route back to the
Visitor Centre.

Access & Parking free

Beinn Ìme and the Arrochar hills

Descending to Shielhill Glen

Kip Water lies in the deep wooded gorge of the Shielhill Glen and provides the focus for this short but delightful nature ramble. The route is suitable for most children, although the very youngest may need some guidance on the waterside path which can be slippery, on the various footbridges over the burn and the long boardwalk ascent to join the Kelly Cut.

From the Greenock Cut Visitor Centre (previously named Cornalees Bridge) at the southern end of the Loch Thom compensation reservoir, follow the road back towards Cornalees Bridge. Just before the bridge turn right onto a path and follow it down to a footbridge.

Cross over and continue on the path with the deep gorge of the Kip Water

Shielhill Glen

opening up on the left and the aqueduct of the **Greenock Cut [19]** on the right. Follow the Greenock Cut to a kissing gate where the path divides. The right-hand path continues alongside the Greenock Cut towards Shielhill Farm, while the left-hand branch

START & FINISH: *Greenock Cut Visitor Centre car park (NS247722)*

DISTANCE: *3km; 1.75 miles*

TIME: *50mins*

MAP: *OS 63*

TERRAIN: *Paths; muddy in places, stepped boardwalk*

GRADE: *Easy*

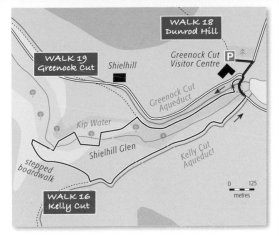

through broadleaf woodland of oak, ash, silver birch and rowan. Assorted small footbridges zigzag back and forth over the burn to finish on the left-hand bank, followed by a larger bridge crossing back to the right-hand bank.

Pass the remains of a sandstone quarry which supplied the building materials for some of Greenock's villas, then over another bridge back to the left-hand bank.

descends towards the Kip Water.

Descend left and a short distance down on the right the concrete foundations of a WWII anti-aircraft gun emplacement provide level support for picnic tables and open views west over green fields to Dunoon and the Clyde.

The burn is soon reached and followed over sections of boardwalk

Beyond this the path moves away from the burn to arrive at a kissing gate. Go through and ascend the long stepped boardwalk across marshy moorland and out of the glen to gain the path beside the **Kelly Cut** [16]. Turn left and follow this back to the car park.

Access & Parking free

Greenock Cut Visitor Centre

Shielhill farm and Dunrod Hill

Overlooking Loch Thom to the west lie the modest summits of Hillside Hill and Dunrod Hill. They aren't high, but their position coupled with the relative flatness of the surrounding moorland makes them prominent in the landscape.

Both hills are easily tackled from the Greenock Cut Visitor Centre (previously named Cornalees Bridge) and can be combined with tracks to the north, to produce a round route with a return beside Loch Thom. The going is rough and boggy in places and while much of the route is on track, the moorland descent from Dunrod Hill is tricky in poor visibility and not recommended in those conditions.

The route starts from the far left-hand corner of the Visitor Centre car park near a Cheetah engine from an Avro Anson aeroplane which crashed near Dunrod Hill in 1939. A second engine lies semi-buried below the drained No1 reservoir north of Dunrod. No other wreckage remains.

From the engine follow a path beside the wall to a stile. Cross over and continue beside the wall to where the route steepens. Here a gentler path can

Avro Anson engine at the Visitor Centre

START & FINISH: *Greenock Cut Visitor Centre car park (NS247722)*

DISTANCE: *6km; 3.75 miles*

TIME: *2hrs*

MAP: *OS 63*

TERRAIN: *Hillwalk, using tracks & paths; boggy in places*

GRADE: *Moderate / Strenuous*

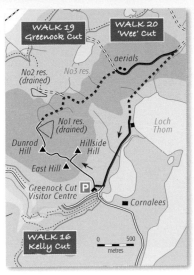

be taken off to the right then back left to gain the col between East Hill and Hillside Hill.

A lesser path leads to the cairned summit of Hillside Hill with views west to the prominent trig point on Dunrod Hill and east over Loch Thom to Hill of Stake and Misty Law.

Descend westwards to the fence and a wooden gate from where a marshy path heads towards Dunrod Hill, passing through a low wall before a short ascent to the summit. The next objective is the boulder and earth dam of the old reservoir, which in good visibility can be seen below and directly to the north.

From the trig point go north then east to re-gain the low wall, a well-worn path and an all-terrain-vehicle track. Pass through a wall junction to gain the old dam of the now drained reservoir, with its incongruous Danger No Swimming notices. Drop down at the dam breach, cross the burn and follow a grassy track north east to a junction. Turn right onto a stony track and follow this to the aerial access road, which is descended to the main track alongside Loch Thom. Turn right and follow the track and road back to the Visitor Centre.

Access & Parking free

East Hill and Hillside Hill above Loch Thom

Greenock Cut

*A*lthough the Greenock Cut aqueduct has been super-seded as the main supplier of fresh water to the Clyde ports, the adjacent walkway has recently been refurbished and offers an enjoyable walk with open views over the Clyde to the mountains. The reservoirs surrounding Loch Thom still provide the water, but since 1971 it has been fed direct via an underground pipe, rather than taking its own steady pace round the hillside. The cut, its surrounding reservoirs (full and drained) and their dams, buildings, sluice mechanisms, drainage channels and footbridges are all scheduled ancient monuments. Inverclyde Council took over the Greenock Cut from Scottish Water in 2005 and have injected significant resources into repairing and main-taining the water channel, walkway, bridges and buildings.

The best direction in which to tackle the route is anti-clockwise. This gets the road and track over and done with at the start and presents the best views over the Clyde to the peaks of the Southern Highlands.

From the Greenock Cut Visitor Centre (previously named Cornalees Bridge) at the southern end of Loch Thom, follow the road north past Ardgowan Fishery to Loch Thom Cottage. Ascend steadily on a track above Loch Thom to where an access road from the aerials up on the left joins the main track. This access road is utilised by the walks over **Hillside Hill & Dunrod Hill** [18] and beside the **'Wee' Cut** [20].

This high point and the track which descends from it, offer good views west and north over the Clyde from Dunoon and the high hills of Cowal to the Arrochar hills, Helensburgh the Luss hills and distant Ben Lomond.

Two small reservoirs are passed to arrive at Overton and a bridge over the

START & FINISH: *Greenock Cut Visitor Centre car park (NS247722)*

DISTANCE: *12km; 7.5 miles*

TIME: *4hrs*

MAP: *OS 63*

TERRAIN: *Roads, tracks & maintained paths*

GRADE: *Moderate*

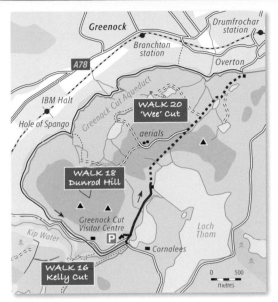

kilometres, gaining just 20 metres in elevation between Overton and Cornalees. This feels like you're walking on the level, but in fact you're walking slightly uphill. The water meanwhile is travelling gently downhill; not fast enough to create a torrent but just enough to keep it moving.

Highlights of the route are further spectacular views south-west to Bute, Kintyre and Arran, workmen's stone bothies and sluice gates designed to prevent the aqueduct overspilling in times of spate, access bridges and the impressively incut ravine of the Hole of Spango overlooking the IBM complex.

cut, the left wall of which holds a drinking fountain commemorating the aqueduct's centenary in 1927.

The walkway beside the aqueduct traverses the hillside for the next eight

Access & Parking free

Start of the Greenock Cut

Looking west from the 'Wee' Cut

While the Greenock Cut is well known and well frequented and the Kelly Cut deserves more visitors than it gets, there is a third aqueduct in the hills above Greenock.

Known as the 'Wee' Cut, this aqueduct is significantly shorter than the others and links the outflow from No3 reservoir with No5 reservoir. It's more of a hillpath than a walkway, but the route is clear and allows the walker to step off the beaten track into wild moorland landscape with panoramic views across the Firth of Clyde.

From the Greenock Cut Visitor Centre (previously named Cornalees Bridge) at the southern end of Loch Thom, follow the road north past Ardgowan Fishery to Loch Thom Cottage. Ascend

Greenock and the Firth of Clyde

the track above Loch Thom almost to its high point and turn left onto an access road leading up to the prominent aerials.

Fantastic views over Greenock and Gourock to the Clyde and the mountains

START & FINISH: Greenock Cut Visitor Centre car park (NS247722)

DISTANCE: 8.5km; 5.25 miles

TIME: 2hrs 50mins

MAP: OS 63

TERRAIN: Roads, tracks & paths; muddy & rough in places

GRADE: Moderate

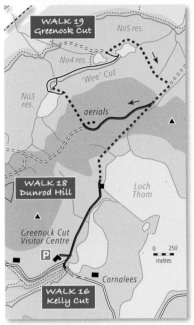

WALK 19 Greenock Cut

No5 res.

No4 res.

'Wee' Cut

No3 res.

aerials

Loch Thom

WALK 18 Dunrod Hill

Greenock Cut Visitor Centre

P

0   250
metres

Cornalees

WALK 16 Kelly Cut

can be had from the track before it starts a steep descent to No3 reservoir. Two routes are possible from the dam. Either leave the track and cross the dam wall and the outflow, from where a path descends round to the right to gain the 'Wee' Cut, or follow the track to where it ends below the dam, from where a path, intermittent at first, leads down right to gain the cut.

Follow the path along the north bank of the 'Wee' Cut past No4 reservoir to the banks of No5. Turn left and skirt No5 to an access track leading left to No4 reservoir. Turn right and follow this track clockwise round No5 and ascend to rejoin the Loch Thom track slightly down from its high point.

Re-ascend to the high point and retrace the outward route back to the Visitor Centre. Combining this route with **Hillside Hill & Dunrod Hill** [18] offers an interesting hill and moorland walk of about 9.5km in total.

Access & Parking free

Number 4 reservoir and the Firth of Clyde

Windy Hill

indy Hill is an excellent outing for younger hill-walkers. The route is interesting, well signposted, well maintained and mostly on the level. Any uphill sections short lived and the boggy bits crossed by boardwalks.

At 316m it's the highest point in Muirshiel Country Park, although significantly lower than Hill of Stake to the west, which at 522m is the highest point of the surrounding Muirshiel Regional Park. Windy Hill stands proud of the surrounding moorland and while this means fine views, it also means it's an exposed spot so wrap up tight. The described route makes the most of the waymarked paths in Muirshiel Country Park and offers an extension off the beaten track to rocky Creag Minnan to the north-east.

From Lochwinnoch follow the B786 north towards Kilmacolm, then the signposted single track road north-west

above the River Calder. Park at the very first car park, which is on the left just inside the white stone gateposts at the entrance to the Country Park. Muirshiel, meaning 'steading on the moor' comes from the name of the farm which stood in this area in the late 1700s.

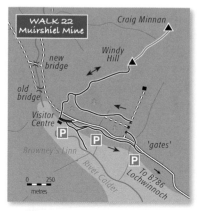

WALK 22
Muirshiel Mine

Craig Minnan

new bridge

Windy Hill

old bridge

Visitor Centre

P

P

Browney's Linn

P

'gates'

To B786 Lochwinnoch

River Calder

0   250
metres

START & FINISH: *Muirshiel Country Park car park (NS319629)*

DISTANCE: *6km; 4 miles*

TIME: *2hrs*

MAP: *OS 63*

TERRAIN: *Paths; mostly waymarked, boggy in places*

GRADE: Easy / *Moderate*

Follow the path from the back of the car park down through Gate Wood, keeping right where it divides to gain the access road. Cross the road and over a burn to reach a farm track and follow that rightwards.

Leave the track at the second waymarked path on the left and follow it through the conifers of Orblis Wood past a replica Bronze Age hut to a wall. On the right an initially faint path leads up through a dark conifer plantation. If you find yourself descending from this wall to a boardwalk then you have overshot this turning.

The path now leads up past Monument Wood, named after an inaccessible granite monument in the wood marking the grave of County Clare MP and politician Lord Francis Conyngham who owned Muirshiel House and died there in 1880. The house, which stood in the vicinity of the present day Visitor Centre, was demolished after Renfrew County Council bought the estate in 1950.

Gain the open hillside at a second

Windy Hill summit

wall and kissing gate, from where a refurbished path and boardwalk lead almost to the summit of Windy Hill. A final grassy ascent brings you to the top and fine views north across the Firth of Clyde to the high hills of the Southern Highlands and south over the River Calder to Lochwinnoch, Castle Semple Country Park [23 & 24] and rural Ayrshire. Small cliffs surround the summit area, so keep an eye on the very young when admiring the view.

At this point the adventurous can descend to the north, cross a fence at a stile and ascend the lower but craggier Craig Minnan for even better views.

Return by the same route over Windy Hill back to the first wall in the woodland and descend on a boardwalk into the forest. The paths become a little confused, but all descend to the Visitor Centre. From the car park left of the centre take the right-hand of two paths which leads down through a picnic and barbecue site to a kissing gate and riverside path by the River Calder to Browney's Linn. Return to the kissing gate, turn right and ascend beside a burn to a traversing path which is followed rightwards through woodland past assorted car parks back to the entrance gate.

Creag Minnan

Access & Parking free

Approaching Muirshiel barytes mine

*A*fter steady decline from peak production in 1945, Muirshiel barytes mine closed in the late 1960s, ending more than 200 years of mineral extraction from the surrounding hills. Ironically, one of the modern uses of this high density mineral (the name originates from the Greek word for heavy), is in oil drilling and local demand was to soar over the next decade with the exploration and exploitation of oil in the North Sea.

Some 0.3 million tons of barytes was extracted from the site, initially in the form of open-cast mining and then via shafts said to be more than 180 metres deep. The primary use for the mineral was in paint and paper manufacture.

The last buildings remained standing until quite recently, but little can be found at the site now save for the 'Muirshiel Mine Shelter' a freight container complete with chairs, which offers an incongruous though welcome shelter for walkers visiting the location. Although the Muirshiel mine no longer

operates, Scotland remains the biggest producer of barytes in the UK, mostly from the Faragon Hill mine near Aberfeldy – a world class source of high quality mineral.

From Lochwinnoch follow the B786 north towards Kilmacolm, then the signposted single track road north-west above the River Calder to the car park at the Visitor Centre where the road ends at a gate. Go through the gate and emerge from the woodland

START & FINISH: *Muirshiel Country Park car park (NS319629)*
DISTANCE: *8.5km; 5.25 miles*
TIME: *2hr 50mins*

MAP: *OS 63*
TERRAIN: *Tracks & paths; boggy in places*
GRADE: *Easy*

the higher Hill of Stake to the north.

Pass the old bridge over the River Calder then cross the new bridge and skirt the heathery flanks of Queenside Hill, with views back to Windy Hill and Craig Minnan. These views and those north to Ben Lomond and the Southern Highlands make this walk: there would be little to commend it in poor visibility.

The track curves round into the upper glen ascending gently to where it divides below the mine workings. Turn left here and ascend straight past the shelter to where the track ends at a fence enclosing the old mine workings. A return can be made back along the track to the Visitor Centre from here, but a path can be followed up the left side of the fence and over the burn to the top of the enclosing fence for a view west to rounded Hill of Stake, before returning to the track.

surrounding the Visitor Centre on an open track ascending the glen.

South-west of the Visitor Centre and across the river, lies the distinct bump of Misty Law. It's the second highest hill in the area, but more prominent than

Access & Parking free

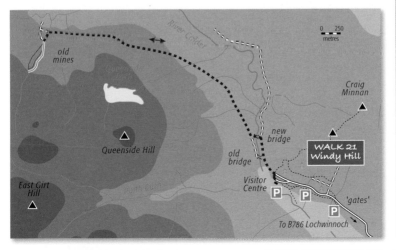

Castle Semple Collegiate Church

astle Semple offers some varied walks combining cycle paths beside the loch and along the track bed of the old railway, with tracks and paths through Parkhill Wood and the ruins of the 16th century Castle Semple Collegiate Church to its east.

From the Visitor Centre car park, accessed from the A760 east of Lochwinnoch or from the village itself, follow the lochside gravel path past the sailing club to the Blackditch Burn, where it swings left and ascends to meet the Glasgow to Irvine cycle path.

Straight ahead is Parkhill Wood , which forms the second half of this walk. Turn right here onto the tarmac cycle path (signposted Kilbarchan and Glasgow) and follow it north-east. Pass under a bridge and beyond a deep cutting, the ruins of the church can be seen in fields on the left. Before crossing the next bridge, descend down

left as signposted to reach a farm track and follow it up left to the church. Founded in 1504 by Lord John Sempill, it was extended to take his impressive monument after Sempill fell at Flodden in 1513. Part of this monument remains, but the church was de-roofed after the Reformation.

Return to the track and continue to a gate at the east end of Parkhill Wood. Turn right immediately after the metal gateposts and boundary fence and descend following yellow waymarks, ignoring a turning on the left and crossing over two burns. Cross back over the second burn to a junction and turn right ascending through silver birch beside a burn.

Cross a footbridge over the Blackditch Burn and continue ascending with a few glimpses south to Parkhill, the high point on the walk. Descend to a junction and continue straight ahead on a pleasant grassy path which swings

START & FINISH: *Castle Semple Country Park car park (NS358591)*

DISTANCE: *7km; 4.25 miles*

TIME: *2hr 20mins*

MAP: *OS 63*

TERRAIN: *Waymarked paths; muddy in places*

GRADE: *Easy*

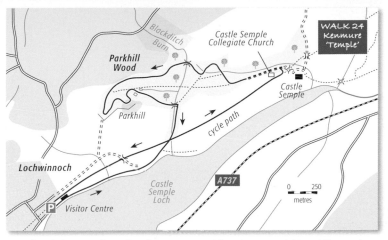

round and rises to a boundary fence and views across to Lochwinnoch. Go over a craggy little top then sharp right to the top of Parkhill and views northwest to Misty Law and the upland of Muirshiel Regional Park.

Descend beside the fence to join a path coming in from the left. At the next junction turn right past the pool and grotto and on to a footbridge over the Blackditch Burn. A right turn here leads back to the wood entrance and the railway cycle path which is followed back to the Visitor Centre.

Access & Parking free

Castle Semple Loch and Visitor Centre

Kenmure Temple

Kenmure Hill with its octagonal stone 'temple' offers fine views south over the three lochs, Castle Semple, Barr and Kilbirnie, and provides the focal point for this pleasant ramble through the Renfrewshire countryside.

Dating from the mid-1700s and at one time surrounded by a walled deer park, the 'temple' is actually an outlook tower built to allow William Macdowall extensive views over his Castle Semple estate; its prominent position reminding the locals of both his power and his wealth. Today the roof has gone, along with the windows and the first floor, but the walls remain.

From the Visitor Centre car park, accessed from the A760 east of Lochwinnoch or from the village itself, follow the gravel path past the sailing club and round Castle Semple Loch to the Blackditch Burn to join the Glasgow to Irvine cycle path. Turn right and follow the tarmac cycle path to just

before a circular tunnel taking the path below the road, where a wooden kissing gate on the right gives access to a grassy track. Follow this round until it is possible to ascend the grassy hillside diagonally left below the line of small cliffs to the tower.

Descend the broad western flanks towards Castle Semple Loch to regain the path and follow it past the ruins of a 19th century laundry and through the remains of the deer park wall to join the path coming in from Garthland Bridge. Turn right here and cross the

START & FINISH: *Castle Semple Country Park car park (NS358591)*

DISTANCE: *7km; 4.25 miles*

TIME: *2hrs 20mins*

MAP: *OS 63*

TERRAIN: *Tracks & paths; some waymarking, muddy in places*

GRADE: *Easy*

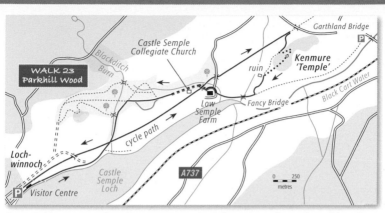

Fancy Bridge over a minor burn to a metal kissing gate and Scottish Rights of Way and Access Society signpost. Alas the bridge is not as fancy as it was having lost its railings.

Continue along the grassy track beside the loch to reach Low Semple Farm. Go through a wooden gate to an access road and follow this round the right side of the house to a junction. Turn left, signposted Low Semple Farm, and follow the road towards the bungalow, then right onto a track. Pass under the bridge (the kissing gate on the left accesses the cycle path) and straight ahead to the 16th century Castle Semple Collegiate Church.

Follow the track into Parkhill Wood and continue round through the woodland to exit at the cycle path, which leads back to the Visitor Centre. If desired a short diversion can be had by taking the first turning on the left after entering Parkhill Wood, which offers a short loop round the high ground south of the main path.

Access & Parking free

Low Semple Farm

Finlaystone house

inlaystone house incorporates parts of older buildings, but mostly dates from the 1760s and 1900s. One-time home of the Earls of Glencairn, the house boasts connections with John Knox and Robert Burns and is currently the family home of the Chief of Clan MacMillan.

Assorted waymarked and unwaymarked paths crisscross the estate and the following description combines the best bits, starting with the woodland and ending with the house and gardens. From the car park and ticket office cross the access road to the bridge over the burn and follow yellow and red waymarks into the woodland where the route divides.

Go right and straight up on the Yellow Scout Trail past the Arboretum path (a short circuit above the loch) and continue steeply up and round through pleasant broadleaf woodland and rhododendron tunnels before descending

to a wall. Keep right and pass through a boggy area with a burn and on through conifers with views south over fields.

Keep well to the right while descending through the conifers beyond to gain a wall and a junction with a yellow waymark pointing left. Turn left – ignore the path which continues straight ahead into broadleaf

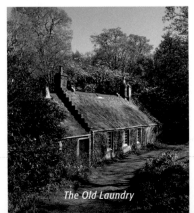

The Old Laundry

START & FINISH: *Finlaystone Country Estate car park (NS365735)*
DISTANCE: *3.5km; 2 miles*
TIME: *1hr 10mins*

MAP: *OS 63*
TERRAIN: *Waymarked paths*
GRADE: *Easy*

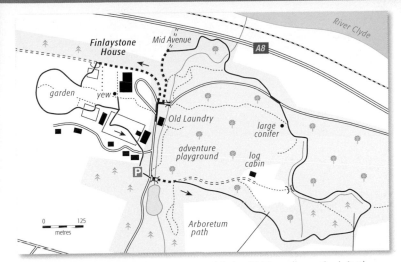

woodland where it fades – and descend beside the small burn. Pass a path coming in from the left (this leads back up through the conifers) to arrive at another junction and a footbridge over the burn; the continuation of the red route which was left at the start.

Do not cross over, but continue beside the burn to its lowest point. Swing left, then straight ahead at the next junction towards a tall conifer tree. Go right here following yellow (the red continues ahead) to gain the access road which leads left, to another path off right. Descend through woodland past another junction towards the northern perimeter of the estate, with noise now discernible from traffic on the A8 to the north. Cross the bridge over the burn to gain Mid Avenue and follow it left to join the access road.

The route now turns right onto a track below the front of the house, but it is worth continuing up the access road to visit the Old Laundry on the left. The daily toil of fire lighting, boiling, bleaching and starching is well displayed with a range of original fittings and an amazing set of fully functioning cast iron drying racks that slide into the wall. Return to the junction and continue straight on following the track round below the front of the house to steps. These lead up to silver gates and access to the sunken garden right of the 'battlement' hedges dividing the private garden from the public garden.

Turn right and follow paths anti-clock-wise round the public garden and through the Knot Garden to the entrance to the walled garden. A short detour down to the left reveals the yew tree where John Knox is said to have delivered communion in 1566. Return through the walled garden and past the cafe to the archway exit to the car park.

Access & Parking charge

Balgray Reservoir

Despite being located in the most populated part of Scotland, the Country Parks in this chapter offer numerous opportunities to swop traffic noise and the urban landscape for secluded river gorges, open moorland and ancient woodland.

However, it's a little harder to totally escape the skyline of Glasgow and the Clyde Valley towns. This is not necessarily a drawback and many of the walks are positively enhanced by spectacular views over the city, backed by the Kilpatrick and Campsie Hills and distant Ben Lomond.

In 1854, Hugh MacDonald stood on Gleniffer Braes and wrote in *Rambles Round Glasgow*, "let us now glance at the picture which is spread before us,

and we verily believe that a fairer one exists not in bonny Scotland". Modern housing now dominates the view but Gleniffer Gorge & The Braes [26] still offers one the best cityscapes in this guidebook. Pick a good day and many landmarks can be identified without the need for binoculars. Glen Park Dams [27] at the base of Gleniffer Braes offer a pleasant family ramble among reservoirs engineered by Robert Thom of **Greenock Cut** [19] fame, as well as access to a new path network on the wilder high ground above Brownside & Fereneze Braes [28].

Known as 'the Dams', the reservoirs between Barrhead, Darnley and Newton Mearns offered recreation to generations prior to 2008, when the

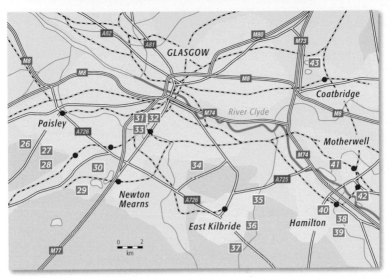

area was formalised as Dams to Darnley Country Park, in a joint initiative between Glasgow and East Renfrewshire Councils. Improved access and new footpaths have followed, with more in the planning. The walks round Balgray Reservoir [29] and Waulkmill Glen [30] link some of these routes with paths and tracks outside the Country Park.

The estate surrounding Pollok House,

William Adam's fine Georgian mansion maintained by the National Trust for Scotland, combines ancient natural woodland, open parkland and playing fields, and the world class Burrell Collection museum and art gallery. A network of formal and informal paths can be utilised for a circumnavigation of the White Cart Water [31], a tour Around The Burrell [32] and its

GLENIFFER BRAES COUNTRY PARK

Located on the southern outskirts of Paisley

Renfrewshire Council
<www.renfrewshire.gov.uk>

Getting There
Foot: *From Glenburn & Foxbar-Paisley; Barrhead*

Road: *From Glasgow & Edinburgh – M8, A726, B774/775. From Stirling –*

M80, M8, A726, B774/775

Train: *Paisley Gilmour Street (4.5km to 5.5km); Barrhead (2km). First ScotRail see p7*

Bus: *See p7*

Facilities
Glen Park: *Information Centre (0141 8843794), toilets*

Countryside Ranger Service: *Walks & educational events*

Other Activities: *Robertson Park children's play area, Orienteering*

DAMS TO DARNLEY COUNTRY PARK

Located between Barrhead, Glasgow & Newton Mearns

East Renfrewshire Council
<www.eastrenfrewshire.gov.uk>

Glasgow Council
<www.glasgow.gov.uk>

Getting There
Foot: *From Barrhead & Darnley-Glasgow*

Road: *From Glasgow M77, A726. From Edinburgh – M8, M77, A726. From Stirling – M80, M8, M77, A726*

Train: *Barrhead, (3km); Priesthill & Darnley-Glasgow (800m). First ScotRail see p7*

Bus: *See p7*

Facilities
Countryside Ranger Service: *Walks & educational events*

Further Information
Website: *<www.damstodarnley.org>*

POLLOK COUNTRY PARK

Located on Glasgow's 'South Side'

Glasgow Council
<www.glasgow.gov.uk>

Getting There
Foot: *From south Glasgow*

Road: *From Glasgow & Edinburgh – M8, M77, B768/9. From Stirling – M80, M8, M77, B768/9*

Train: *Shawlands-Glasgow, (680m); Pollokshaws West-Glasgow (200m). First ScotRail see p7*

Bus: *See p7*

Facilities
Countryside Rangers' Visitor Centre: *(0141 6329299), toilets*

Burrell Collection: *(0141 6497151), art collection, toilets*

Pollok House: *(0141 6166410), 18th century house & grounds maintained by National Trust for Scotland, toilets*

Countryside Ranger Service: *Walks & educational events*

Other Activities: *Adventure playground, orienteering courses, mountain bike courses*

Food, Drink & Shops: *Burrell Collection & Pollok House (cafe-restaurants, gifts, arts & crafts)*

Further Information
National Trust for Scotland
<www.nts.org.uk>

CATHKIN BRAES COUNTRY PARK

Located on the south-eastern edge of Glasgow

Glasgow Council
<www.glasgow.gov.uk>

Getting There
Foot: *From Castlemilk-Glasgow & Carmunnock*

Road: *From Glasgow A730, A749, B759. From Edinburgh – M8, M73, M74, A749, B759. From Stirling – M80, M73, M74, A749, B759*

Train: *Burnside-Glasgow (2.5km). First ScotRail see p7*

Bus: *See p7*

Facilities
Countryside Ranger Service: *Walks & educational events*

Other Activities: *Orienteering courses, mountain bike courses*

Pollok Park

purpose-built gallery and through the great North Wood [33].

The elevated Cathkin Braes define Glasgow's south-eastern boundary, with the ancient Big Wood & Wind Law [34] offering spectacular views across the city to the Highlands beyond.

The next eight walks lie south and east of Glasgow and feature the River Clyde and its tributaries; the Rotten Calder and River Avon (named Avon Water on Ordnance Survey maps) to the south and South Calder Water to the north. All of these rivers are characterised by deep wooded gorges cut through the sedimentary coal-bearing beds which form the bedrock of central Scotland. The routes here are all in long-standing Country Parks with an extensive network of well-maintained and well-signposted paths.

The Rotten Calder [35] with its many waterfalls can be explored from Calderglen Country Park near East Kilbride and via The Tor & South Bridge [36], while the route south to Langlands Moss [37] local nature reserve runs alongside the Calder Water.

Another William Adam creation, the magnificent Chatelherault near Hamilton, offers routes Beside The River Avon [38] to the Green Bridge & Cadzow Oaks [39] and the Duke's Monument [40]. The gnarled Cadzow Oaks are thought to be between 600 and 900 years old, while the rather less impressive man-made monument commemorates the 11th Duke of Hamilton, whose grave is visited on the walk through **Cnocan Gorge** [1] at Brodick Castle on the Isle of Arran. Chatelherault is all that remains of the Duke of Hamilton's Palace and formal park.

South Calder Water [41] offers an interesting and pleasant walk taking in a modern funfair, a Roman Bath House and a high railway viaduct and is easily accessed from Strathclyde Country Park beside the M74. However, the main focus for the park is the extensive man-made Strathclyde Loch with its variety of watersports. The park also offers

CALDERGLEN COUNTRY PARK

Located at East Kilbride

South Lanarkshire Council
<www.southlanarkshire.gov.uk>

Getting There

Foot: *From East Kilbride*

Road: *From Glasgow M77, A726. From Edinburgh – M8, M77, A726. From Stirling – M80, M8, M77, A726*

Train: *East Kilbride (3km). First ScotRail see p7*

Bus: *See p7*

Facilities

Visitor Centre: *(01355 236644), toilets*

Countryside Ranger Service: *Walks & educational events*

Other Activities: *Children's zoo, conservatory & gardens, orienteering courses, adventure playground*

Food, Drink & Shops: *Visitor Centre (cafe, gifts, arts & crafts)*

Further Information

Langlands Moss Local Nature Reserve: *<www.folm-ek.org.uk>*

CHATELHERAULT COUNTRY PARK

Located on the south-eastern edge of Hamilton

South Lanarkshire Council
<www.southlanarkshire.gov.uk>

Getting There

Foot: *Easy access from Hamilton*

Road: *From Glasgow M8, M74, A723, A72. From Edinburgh – M8, M73, M74, A723, A72. From Stirling – M80, M73, M74, A723, A72*

Train: *Chatelherault (750m); Hamilton Central (2km), First ScotRail see p7*

Bus: *See p7*

Facilities

Visitor Centre: *(01698 426213), toilets*

Countryside Ranger Service: *Walks & educational events*

Adventure Playground: *Near Visitor Centre*

Food, Drink & Shops: *Visitor Centre (cafe, gifts), garden centre*

STRATHCLYDE COUNTRY PARK

Located between Motherwell & Hamilton

North Lanarkshire Council
<www.northlanarkshire.gov.uk>

Getting There

Foot: *From Motherwell & Hamilton*

Road: *From Glasgow M8, M74, A725. From Edinburgh – M8, M73, M74, A725. From Stirling – M80, M73, M74, A725*

Train: *Motherwell (1.5km); Airbles (1.5km) First ScotRail see p7*

Bus: *See p7*

Facilities

Countryside Ranger Service: *Walks & educational events*

Other Activities: *Orienteering courses, sailing, canoeing, wind-surfing, waterskiing etc. Instruction and hire (01698 402060).*

M&D's Theme Park: *<www.scotlandsthemepark.com>*

Further Information

Dalzell Estate: *<www.northlanark-shire.gov.uk>*

Baron's Haugh: *<www.rspb.org.uk>*

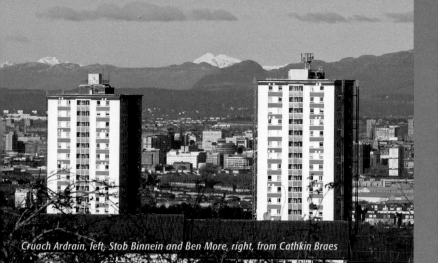

Cruach Ardrain, left, Stob Binnein and Ben More, right, from Cathkin Braes

easy access to a longer route south beside the River Clyde Walkway to the RSPB Barons Haugh [42] Nature Reserve and the council-maintained footpaths surrounding the 16th century Dalzell House – at one time another Hamilton stronghold. Another massive, twisted oak in the grounds of the house is said to have been planted by David I in the mid-1100s.

The final walk in this chapter is at Drumpellier Country Park on the outskirts of Coatbridge. Lochend & Monkland [43] takes in the natural Lochend Loch, a water filled 'kettle hole' formed during the ice age, and the remaining section of the man-made Monkland Canal.

DRUMPELLIER COUNTRY PARK

Located at Coatbridge

North Lanarkshire Council
<www.northlanarkshire.gov.uk>

Getting There
Foot: *Easy access from Coatbridge*

Road: *From Glasgow & Edinburgh M8, A89, A752. From Stirling – M80, M73, A89, A752*

Train: *Blairhill (800m). First ScotRail see p7*

Bus: *See p7*

Facilities
Visitor Centre: *(01236 422257), toilets*

Countryside Ranger Service: *Walks & educational events*

Other Activities: *Boat hire, bird watching, ornamental gardens & nursery*

Food & Drink: *Visitor Centre cafe*

Gleniffer Gorge & The Braes

Stanely Reservoir and castle, left, the Kilpatrick Hills and Ben Lomond

"Let us now glance at the picture which is spread before us, and we verily believe that a fairer one exists not in bonny Scotland. At our feet is the old Castle of Stanley, with its sheet of water glittering in the sun; beyond is the magnificent basin of the Clyde, stretching away to the Campsie and Kilpatrick Hills, with all its garniture of woods and fields, mansions and farms, villages and towns, set down as in a map."
Hugh MacDonald, *Rambles Round Glasgow*, 1854

MacDonald wrote these words from the Gleniffer Braes and while his rural tranquillity has been replaced by more than 150 years of urbanisation, the principal elements of the landscape remain. The sun still glints off the reservoir surrounding Stanely Castle and the Clyde basin stretches away over houses and fields to the Kilpatricks and Campsies; everything changes, but nothing changes.

The 'Bonnie Wee Well' at the base of the braes was also immortalised by MacDonald during his Gleniffer ramble and the current well carries his portrait and his poetry, although it's a more rustic version of the ornate original, which was moved to Glasgow Green in 1881 after being vandalised.

Robert Tannahill, weaver poet of Paisley, also roamed the braes and is commemorated in the Tannahill Walk and Tannahill's Well, visited from the Glen Park Dams [27].

Exit from Robertson car park and cross Gleniffer Road onto a path sign-posted Brandy Burn. Follow the main path round with good views over to Ben Lomond, then head left towards conifer plantations and a firebreak. Turn right at the junction and continue to clear the trees, then left below pylon wires to gain the trig point.

Facing Ben Lomond, descend diagonally left to gain a lower path and follow it below the woodland edge veering right where the path divides, to descend below the plantation past old concrete marker blocks.

Go through a tongue of conifers and drop down right to gain a well-worn path, leading to a kissing gate at the edge of Bardrain Wood. Turn left here

START & FINISH: *Robertson Park car park (NS455606)*

DISTANCE: *7km; 4.25 miles*

TIME: *2hrs 20mins*

MAP: *OS 64*

TERRAIN: *Paths; some signposts*

GRADE: *Easy / Moderate*

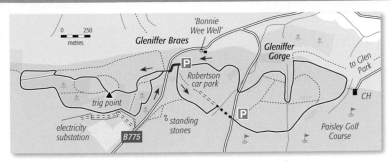

and ascend to the conifer boundary and follow it round towards the electricity substation. Follow the path round the perimeter fence past two gates and into woodland. Pass the firebreak and on to where the fence turns sharp right. Go left here and follow a path through the woodland, right, then left, to a junction. Go left and climb to a high point with a picnic bench and fine views. Turn right, follow the path down and cross the road back to Robertson car park.

Turn right in the car park and up through an old pedestrian gate into open meadow, carpeted with wild flowers in summer. Keep right where the grassy paths divide, swinging round left past a solitary tree to meet a track leading to the car park on Sergeant Law Road.

Pass through a metal kissing gate and follow the boundary of Paisley Golf Club down past the club house to the crest of the braes and a large wooden post with horseshoes and follow the path heading off to the left. Contour the braes west to gain a tarmac path beside Gleniffer Gorge. Turn left and follow the tarmac and earth path up and over the gorge then back down the other side, before heading west to reach Sergeant Law Road again.

Cross over and go right on a good path signposted Tannahill Walkway, Robertson Park and Brandy Burn Way, which leads back to the car park.

Access & Parking free

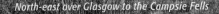

North-east over Glasgow to the Campsie Fells

Glen Park Dams

Lower Reservoir

Paisley's weaver poet Robert Tannahill is forever linked to the Gleniffer Braes, although he wouldn't recognise much of the current Glen Park which centres on two small reservoirs created in the late 1830s, more than 25 years after the poet's death, with engineering assistance from Robert Thom and his nephew James; builders of the **Greenock Cut [19]**.

However there's a good chance he'd recognise the waterfall east of the reservoirs, where the Glen Burn shoots over an overhanging cliff and thunders onto the rocks below. Nearby is Tannahill's Well, erected in the 1850s by William Fulton, owner of the Glen and nearby Glenfield Scouring Works, who built a mansion-house (now demolished) above the lower reservoir.

History records that Fulton was happy for Paisley people to walk the glen and braes and allowed regular fund-raising concerts in the glen where audiences of 30,000 were entertained by choirs of up to 700 voices celebrating Tannahill's birth and works.

Start at the car park off Glenfield Road

START & FINISH: *Glen Park car park (NS480608)*

DISTANCE: *2km; 1.25 miles*

TIME: *40mins*

MAP: *OS 64*

TERRAIN: *Waymarked tracks & paths; muddy in places*

GRADE: *Easy*

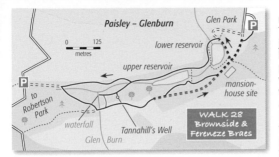

Paisley – Glenburn

Glen Park

lower reservoir

upper reservoir

mansion-house site

to Robertson Park

waterfall

Tannahill's Well

Glen Burn

0 125 metres

WALK 28 Brownside & Fereneze Braes

and follow the path at the back of the car park to gain a tarmac track leading up and right to above the first reservoir. Turn right and follow the gravel track down, then left across a small grassy area. Cross the dam retaining the lower reservoir and a wooden bridge over the outflow, then immediately left, keeping right when the path divides (the left-hand path just circles the reservoir). Continue straight ahead along the north side of the upper reservoir to a junction point where the path divides.

Turn left and follow the wooded Glen Burn past Tannahill's Well to the impressive waterfall. From here steps lead to the upper path, but this misses out a pleasant section of the route, so

retrace the route past Tannahill's Well to the junction and turn left, back onto the main path. Pass through woodland, with the waterfall visible and audible over on the left, to arrive at a left turn. Continuing ahead gains a track leading to the road to Paisley Golf Club and a car park at the start of the Tannahill Walkway onto the Gleniffer Braes. Don't follow this, but go left and ascend through a tunnel of trees, crossing left over the Glen Burn at the top. Shortly afterwards, keep left where the path divides – the right-hand route is taken by Brownside & Fereneze Braes [28] – and continue on past a sign pointing down left to the waterfall.

Gain the tarmac track and either follow this all the way back to the car park, or after a short distance, drop down left to a rougher lower path which joins the tarmac path further on.

Access & Parking free

Beside the Glen Burn

Campsie Fells from Glenburn Reservoir

Brownside Braes and Fereneze Braes flank the eastern side of the Country Park and offer a much wilder moorland experience than Gleniffer Gorge & The Braes [26] and the Glen Park Dams [27].

The route can be reached from the car park at Brownside, but Glen Park off Glenfield Road offers a more enjoyable starting point. A path leads south from the car park to open ground and a tarmaced track through woodland above the reservoirs. When the tarmac ends, continue on the path through more open country passing a signpost indicating a route down right to the Glen Burn waterfall.

Cross over the Glen Burn, then swing left at the next junction where a sign points down and right to the Robertson car park. Ascend a path through woodland to exit onto a track (the continuation of the access road to Paisley Golf Club) and follow that up and left to a gate. The main track swings left to Glenburn Reservoir, but continue straight ahead on a grassy track, the old coach route to Kilmarnock, to the ruins of Braehead Farm and the best standing stone on the braes.

Return to the junction and on to Glenburn Reservoir which is skirted outside the fencing to a wooden footbridge over the Knockindon Burn. Don't cross over, but follow a path on the right side of the burn, which leads to a kissing gate.

Standing stone by Braehead Farm ruins

START & FINISH: *Glen Park car park (NS480608)*

DISTANCE: *7.5km; 4.5 miles*

TIME: *2hrs 30mins*

MAP: *OS 64*

TERRAIN: *Tracks & paths; some waymarking, boggy & rough in places*

GRADE: *Moderate / Strenuous*

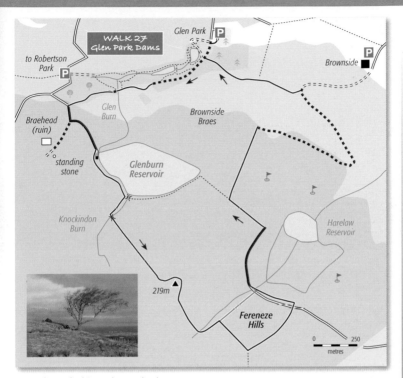

WALK 27
Glen Park Dams

Glen Park

to Robertson Park

Brownside

Braehead (ruin)

Glen Burn

Brownside Braes

standing stone

Glenburn Reservoir

Knockindon Burn

Harelaw Reservoir

219m

Fereneze Hills

0   250
metres

Go through this and over the burn and ascend directly, passing below pylon wires to a few trees and a cairn marking Point 219 metres. Continue round and down to the right to another kissing gate. This path can be followed down to the Harelaw Reservoir access road, but a right turn right leads over a boardwalk and along a long double fence corridor. Where this ends and the path veers to the right, go left through double gates and follow a stony path over the crest to a kissing gate and the reservoir access road. Follow this left to where it ends at a kissing gate at the edge of the now mostly drained Harelaw Reservoir. Turn left onto a path back to Glenburn Reservoir. Just over the crest, turn right signposted Paisley and descend between the wall and fence to gain a track on the right.

Descend this over Brownside Braes with panoramic views north and east over the city, to a sharp right bend. Turn left here – the right-hand route descends to Brownside farm – and follow the signposted route back to Glen Park.

Access & Parking free

81

Littleton Reservoir

Scotland's most recent Country Park was created in 2008 in a joint venture between Glasgow and East Renfrewshire councils and centres round five reservoirs on the high ground south of the city, between Barrhead and Newton Mearns.

A gated tarmac access road links the reservoirs offering visitors generally vehicle-free walking and cycling. Various paths have been developed with more planned and the following walk is mostly on new paths, but with a short section around a field edge.

A new car park on Balgraystone Road at the east end of Balgray Reservoir, is easily reached from Barrhead (signposted from Springhill Road, before St Luke's High School) and offers the easiest access. Limited parking is also possible at a small layby on Aurs Road between Barrhead and Newton Mearns, although care is needed as the road is busy and turning

impossible.

From the car park on Balgraystone Road, turn left and follow the main path clockwise round the reservoir. Leave the main path when it starts to veer off left towards the bridge over the railway line, to gain a clear waterside path continuing round the reservoir. This brings you round to a metal scaffolding fence before the dam and a track on

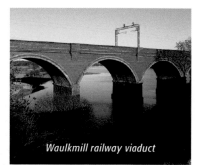

Waulkmill railway viaduct

START & FINISH: *Car park on Balgraystone Road (NS507572)*

DISTANCE: *6km; 3.75 miles*

TIME: *2hrs*

MAP: *OS 64*

TERRAIN: *Roads, tracks & paths; muddy in places*

GRADE: *Easy / Moderate*

Barrhead

St Luke's High School

Springhill Road

WALK 30
Waulkmill Glen

Waulkmill Glen Res.

Littleton Res.

Aurs Road

Balgraystone Road

P

P

Balgray Reservoir

Ryat Linn Reservoir

0   125
metres

M77

the left which leads to Aurs Road.

Cross the road and over the gate on the other side and follow the left edge of the field to gain a field track which leads down and through a bridge under the railway. The track turns right then left on a long straight leading up to trees. Follow the track right but continue straight ahead around the field to a wall and ruins, from where a path leads to a bridge over the waterway.

Turn right and follow the road alongside Waulkmill Glen and Ryat Linn Reservoirs to a junction by a waterfall. Turning right here leads up to the layby on Aurs Road. Turn left and ascend to the main road. Cross over and follow the path right the way round Balgray Reservoir. The reservoir is popular with anglers and offers fine open views to the surrounding countryside.

Access & Parking free

Ryat Linn Reservoir

Brock Burn pond

Waulkmill Glen and the Brock Burn are the main focus of the southern section of the Country Park, where the high ground containing the reservoirs descends to Darnley on the southern edge of Glasgow. The first reservoirs date from the 1850s, built by the Gorbals Gravitation Water Company to supply southern parts of the city with clean water via the Brock Burn; the associated filter beds, sluice gates and buildings can still be found at the head of Waulkmill Glen.

The glen itself has a number of paths well used by locals, but there is no waymarking, so a little route finding is required. The remainder of the walk takes in agricultural open meadow south of Darnley Mains and the retail park.

There is no dedicated car park but parking is permitted at the Ashoka Restaurant and the surrounding shops and residential areas offer other parking possibilities. From the park entrance on Nitshill Road, follow the path to a stone

Waulkmill Reservoir

START & FINISH: *Corselet Road, Darnley (NS529595)*

DISTANCE: *6.5km; 4 miles*

TIME: *2hrs 10mins*

MAP: *OS 64*

TERRAIN: *Roads, tracks & paths; muddy in places*

GRADE: *Easy / Moderate*

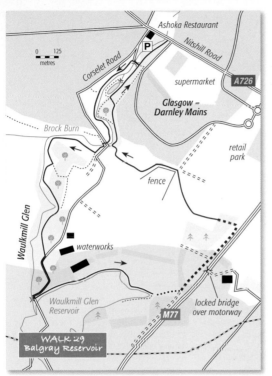

Keeping right at all major junctions, follow the ascending path through the woodland via wooden steps, boardwalks and small wooden footbridges to exit onto Corselet Road.

Turn right and continue up the road until a final zigzag gains the dam wall retaining Waulkmill Glen Reservoir. Go left and follow the road then path clockwise round the reservoir past the old filter beds to the furthest tip of the reservoir. Descend to the fence and go over and cross the small field to a gate which accesses a track beside the M77.

Go left on the track and follow it down and round below the woodland to where this ends, then descend diagonally left over open ground to the corner of the housing estate. Turn left over a stile in the fence and follow a well-worn path round the back of the houses to emerge on a prepared path.

Turn right and follow this to where it starts to pass behind the houses, then drop down left onto a grassy path leading to the pond passed at the start. Go round the pond on either side and continue past the stone bridge back to the park entrance.

bridge and cross over. Turn left beside the Brock Burn and past the pond to where the path makes a zigzag descent to exit onto Corselet Road. Turn left then immediately right and ascend to a raised bank topped by a path.

Cross the culvert over the Brock Burn and continue to shortly before the path ends, where a well-worn path heads rightwards across a meadow. Avoiding all deviations to the river follow this path round, then left towards an old orange gate and pass easily through the fence to its right into woodland.

Access & Parking free

Pollok House

oted Best Park in Britain 2007 and Europe's Best Park the following year, Pollok offers a mixture of recreational and cultural activities unmatched anywhere else in Scotland. The purpose-built glass, stone and steel gallery housing Sir William Burrell's diverse collection of art, sculpture, stained glass, amour and up-market bric-a-brac is matched by Pollok House, with its extensive gardens, Clydesdale horses and works by El Greco, Goya and Blake.

Surrounding them is Pollok Estate, a mixture of farmland, playing fields, open grassland and mature woodland, crisscrossed by a mixture of tracks, paths and cycle routes.

The following short route circles the White Cart Water, finishing with an exploration of the gardens. From the car park beyond Pollok House, follow the path through woodland beside the White Cart Water to the park road in front of the Pollok House. Cross the footbridge over the river to a track which offers views across to the house and stables as it gains height, before passing through woodland to emerge at a practice area for Pollok Golf Club. Continue down past Pollokshaws Bowling Club and under the rail bridge to Pollokshaws Road.

Turn left past Pollokshaws West railway station and back over the White Cart to the entrance to Pollok Park. Follow the pavement through the gateway then veer left past the tennis court car park to the tarmac cycle path alongside the river. This wooded riverside path leads round to the back of Pollok House gardens which can be entered through the wall before the stables. However, before entering, continue round to the stables, home to Pollok's Clydesdale heavy horses.

Return to the garden and explore at will to arrive at the upper glasshouses. Ascend stone steps right of the

START & FINISH: *Pollok House car park (NS548619)*

DISTANCE: *4km; 2.5 miles*

TIME: *1hr 20mins*

MAP: *OS 64*

TERRAIN: *Roads, tracks & paths*

GRADE: *Easy*

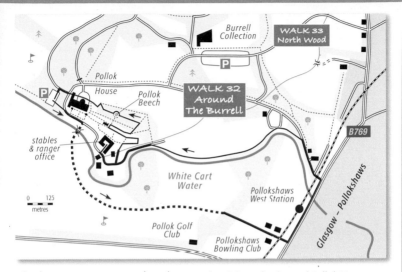

glasshouses to an upper path and follow it right. Go left at the next junction then right and uphill to a stone urn at a path junction. Turn left here and follow the path to the massive Pollok Beech. Continue past the tree and down to the formal garden to exit on the right to the front of Pollok House. Walk down left past the house and exit from the archway to the road and car park beyond.

Access & Parking free
Parking charge at Burrell Collection

White Cart Water

Burrell Collection

In 1944 Sir William Burrell gifted his massive collection of more than 8,000 art objects and collectables to Glasgow. The problem was where to display it and fruitless searching followed. A possible venue didn't appear until 1966 when the Maxwell family gifted Pollok House and Estate to the city after 700 years of occupation. Pollok solved the problem. The winning design for the gallery was chosen in 1971 and the Burrell Collection opened in 1983.

The connection between Burrell and the Maxwells was not a coincidence. Scotland's largest conservation charity, the National Trust for Scotland, of which Sir John Maxwell was a founding member, was conceived at Pollok House in 1931 and the NTS had been involved in the estate since 1939. Today the NTS is still involved, maintaining Pollok House on the council's behalf.

From the car park beyond Pollok House, follow the path through woodland beside the White Cart Water to the park road in front of the house and turn left into the formal gardens at the front of Pollok House. Go through the 'outhouse' at the far right-hand corner and head right across grass to the Rose Garden from where a footbridge leads into the flower and kitchen gardens.

Explore these then return to the right side of the upper glasshouses. Ascend stone steps right of the glasshouses to an upper path and follow it right. Go left at the next junction then right and

START & FINISH: *Pollok House car park (NS548619)*

DISTANCE: *4.5km; 2.75 miles*

TIME: *1hr 30mins*

MAP: *OS 64*

TERRAIN: *Roads, tracks & paths*

GRADE: *Easy*

House and the access road. Turn right and follow the path beside the road, veering left and round to the Burrell Collection.

Continue down past the gallery to a path leading up left and follow this to a junction. Turn right here and round to a footbridge over a burn and another junction. Continue ahead and right to gain the tarmac park road leading from the North Lodge. Turn left and remain on the road round past the pond and the North Wood to emerge on the main access road

uphill to a stone urn at a path junction. Turn left here and follow the path to the massive Pollok Beech. Continue past the tree and down to the formal garden to exit on the right to the front of Pollok

facing Pollok House. Turn right and follow the road back to the car park.

Access & Parking free
Parking charge at Burrell Collection

Burrell Collection

North Wood

Pollok's North Wood covers the highest section of the park and offers a wilder walk away from the wider network of tarmac and prepared paths. A plan by Glasgow Council to develop part of the woods for an aerial ropeway was abandoned after protests and North Wood remains off the beaten track for most visitors.

From the car park beyond Pollok House, follow the path through woodland beside the White Cart Water to the tarmac road in front of the house and follow it down past the Clydesdale heavy horse stables and the ranger office to the walled entrance into the garden. Explore at will to arrive at the upper glasshouses then ascend stone steps right of the glasshouses to an upper path and follow it right. Go left at the next junction then right and uphill to a stone urn at a path junction. Turn

left here and follow the path to the massive Pollok Beech. This distorted tree is thought to be about 250 years old, although how it got to look like this isn't exactly known.

Continue past the tree and down to the formal garden to exit on the right to the front of Pollok House and the access road. Follow the path on the left-hand side of the road, continuing ahead where the road swings left to the Burrell, to a path just down from the road. Cross over an access road and on to just beyond the tennis courts, where a tarmac path goes off left signposted Burrell Collection.

Follow this a short distance, then turn right on a gravel path down a tree-lined avenue. Turn left at the end and continue to Nether Pollok playing fields, skirting the pavilion and car park on the left to gain a track and footbridge over a

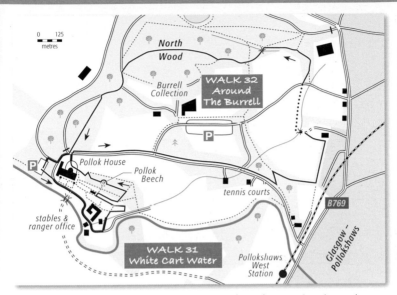

START & FINISH: *Pollok House car park (NS548619)*	**MAP:** *OS 64*
DISTANCE: *4.5km; 2.75 miles*	**TERRAIN:** *Roads, tracks & paths; muddy in places*
TIME: *1hr 30mins*	**GRADE:** *Easy / Moderate*

burn. Head diagonally right across the grass (this can be very wet), to gain a tarmac path starting from the furthest point of the access road.

Go left where the path divides, then left at a footbridge over a small burn.

Ascend to a four-way junction and continue ahead to the edge of North Wood. Leave the tarmac for a path through the trees keeping to the high ground, then veer off to the left and zigzag down to meet the park road. Turn left then second left – the first left is a park road – onto an earth path leading up through rhododendron bushes.

This path, muddy in places, leads to a high point and a view down to Pollok House. The tree-lined avenue nicely frames William Adam's original 'cosy' Georgian country house, slicing off the well-balanced but grandiose wings added in 1892. Descend to the house and follow the access road round right to the car park.

Access & Parking free
Parking charge at Burrell Collection

Big Wood, Cathkin Braes

Forming part of the high ground surrounding Glasgow to the south, Cathkin Braes offer a spectacular panorama over the city with extensive views from the peaks of Arran to the Southern Highlands.

At the eastern end of the rocky escarpment is Queen Mary's Seat where ill-fated Mary Stuart is said to have watched the disastrous battle of Langside in May 1558. The surrounding woodland is marked on William Roy's military map of the mid-1700s and named Caskin hill.

The southern boundary of the Country Park is defined by Cathkin Road and a large car park at its southern end offers the best starting point. From its right-hand end follow a prepared path parallel to the road heading towards the aerial sticking above Big Wood to the north.

At a junction on the woodland edge the path continues beside the road, but

a quieter route can be enjoyed by following the track left for about 65 metres to an earth path on the right leading into the woodland. Follow this to a larger path, continuing ahead and keeping left at any main divisions, until the aerial and its buildings come into sight on the left. It is possible to drop down to the aerial, but pleasanter to continue in the woodland, crossing over a burn to regain the main path and exit onto the grass at Queen Mary's Seat.

At 192m, the trig point below the aerial marks the highest point within the city boundary and offers an unrestricted view of Glasgow's landmarks against a backdrop of Ben Lomond, Stob Binnein, Ben More and Ben Ledi.

Descend a gully in the escarpment and veer left to a lower path. Keep left where it divides and go through a wall to another division. Down and right gives a loop path with an open prospect over

START & FINISH: _Cathkin Road car park (NS610579)_

DISTANCE: _7.5km; 4.5 miles_

TIME: _2hrs 30mins_

MAP: _OS 64_

TERRAIN: _Paths; some tarmac with signposts, muddy in places_

GRADE: _Easy / Moderate_

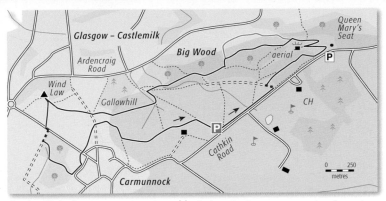

Castlemilk, before an ascent past an old stone gatepost to the main path in Big Wood. However, continue left on the higher path to another division. The right-hand route, perhaps the most interesting of the three options, continues along the crest of the braes to join the loop path, while the left-hand route becomes the main path into Big Wood,

Once back on the main path through Big Wood, follow it on past a path leading back left to the car park. Shortly after crossing the burn, leave the woodland for the prepared path on the left and follow this to a junction. Turn left towards the car park, then right onto a grassy field path to the top of Gallowhill. Descend the other side to cross a tarmac path from Carmunnock village, and ascend another grassy path to the trig point on Wind Law (138m).

Return to the hill crest, then descend diagonally right to a metal field gate on Carmunnock Road. Cross over onto a path between hedges, Pedmyre Lane, and follow this for 60 metres to the entrance to Carmunnock Coppice Woodland on the left. Follow the burn then ascend though woodland to skirt

below the houses to a pedestrian gate on the village edge. Cross Carmunnock Road and follow a grassy field path to a gap in the hedge. Re-cross the tarmac path and ascend towards Gallowhill, veering right near the top to gain another grassy path heading back towards the east end of Carmunnock.

Go through a gap in a hedge, then left above a marshy area to gain the main path leading back to the car park.

Access & Parking free

Ben Lomond from Cathkin Braes

Trough Linn

By far the longest walk described in Calderglen, this route follows the Rotten Calder north to the Hamilton Expressway, then returns to the Country Park via Calderside Road.

The homeward journey offers good views over East Kilbride and the surrounding countryside. Although the walking is on the tarmac surface, traffic visibility is good and the road is not busy. However, the final section at Newhousemill Road is busier and requires more care. An alternative route across a nearby field (within the Country Park boundary) is described here and avoids some of this junction.

From the car park head past the zoo and conservatory and turn left following signs to nature trails and the adventure playground. Go through a red barrier and descend past the adventure playground to a path alongside the Rotten Calder. Follow the path over the river at the Kingfisher footbridge to the road at Newhousemill Bridge.

Cross over and right, onto a wider section of path along the west bank of the river, remaining on the main path as it curves up left towards houses. Don't exit here, but keep right following the sign for Castle Falls and ascend a flight of stairs to the rear of an industrial estate and a sign to an exit at Inch Marnock.

Drop down right and on towards Trough Linn and Black Linn, the first of a series of falls on the river. These are all accessed via loop paths down to the right, which then regain the main path, and are worth the diversion. More housing is then reached and an exit to Inch Keith, followed by a small foot-bridge over a burn with the murky pool of Fred's Pond straight ahead. Turn right and follow a short section of path for a view of the river, before returning to the junction and continuing left to a sign-posted exit to Calderglen Road.

Go right at this point and onto another loop path. Keep right for the series of cascades making up Castle

START & FINISH: Calderglen Country Park car park (NS653527)

DISTANCE: 11.5km; 7 miles

TIME: 3hrs 50mins

MAP: OS 64

TERRAIN: Roads, tracks & paths; muddy in places

GRADE: Easy / Moderate

Map labels:
Hamilton Expressway
A725
Basket Farm
Calderglen House (ruin)
aerial
East Kilbride
Castle Falls
aerial
Fred's Pond
Calderside House
Rotten Calder
Black Linn
Trough Linn
aerial
ruin
aerial
Newhousemill Road
A726
Edge Farm
P
Visitor Centre
Rotten Burn
WALK 37
Langlands Moss
0   500
metres

Falls to re-join the main path and continue to a junction with a route going off to the left. Go down and round to the right here to cross a small bridge and arrive at the site of ruined Calderwood Castle.

Continue to gain a track junction signposted left to Calderwood Gardens and right to Hamilton Expressway. Follow the track to gain the Expressway and follow the pavement right to a turning onto a minor road - Brownrigg Road. Ascend the hairpin bend and follow the road past the farm road to the main junction at Calderside Road.

This is now followed without deviation, passing assorted aerials and Calderside House and farm, to where the road starts to descend towards its junction with the main Newhousemill Road. Just before the main road (there is another aerial at the junction) go through a metal farm gate on the right and follow the field edge beside a burn to pass under power lines towards a ruined building. Just before this a grassy path leads left though a field boundary then diagonally down and right, keeping above a lower marshy area, to gain a metal gate and wooden stile. These access a short section of old track leading to the road. Cross the road with great care and follow it down right to Newhousemill Bridge and the path back to the Visitor Centre.

Access & Parking free

Calderside House

South beside the Rotten Calder

Calderglen offers an excellent and well-maintained network of paths alongside the deep wooded river valley of the Calder Water and Rotten Calder, from Langlands to the A725 expressway.

This walk sticks within the environs of the Visitor Centre and the immediate river banks to give a shorter circuit than Rotten Calder [35] and Langlands Moss [37], and is easily combined with a visit to the hot house conservatory, children's zoo and cafe and the impressive adventure playground.

The route begins with the waymarked Tor Trail, which starts from the corner of the car park diagonally across from the zoo and conservatory, beside the Country Park exit road. Follow the prepared gravel path through rhododendrons and silver birch to conifers and mixed woodland to a footbridge over a burn below

the Tor – a man made earth mound or motte of uncertain date. Cross another footbridge and continue to emerge at the access road and a bridge over the larger Kelvin Burn. Turn left, cross over the bridge, then right back onto the waymarked path.

This is a bit muddier and narrower than the previous section, but leads round through woodland beside the burn with views north over fields to the houses and high flats of East Kilbride.

Cross a bridge back over a burn and descend steps to join the red-waymarked route coming in from the right. Turn right, descend steps, cross another footbridge over the Kelvin Burn and continue to where the yellow and red routes divide. Turn down left to Torrance Linn on the Rotten Calder and follow the path near the river, round below the adventure playground.

START & FINISH: Calderglen
Country Park car park (NS653527)
DISTANCE: 3.5km; 2 miles
TIME: 1hr 10mins

MAP: OS 64
TERRAIN: Waymarked paths
GRADE: Easy

Ascend slightly to a junction and turn left down to the bridge over the Rotten Calder at Horseshoe Falls. Cross over and follow the east bank of the river to steps leading down to the South Bridge. Cross over, ascend to the west bank and follow the path rightwards through woodland back to the Visitor Centre.

Access & Parking free

Above the Rotten Calder

Old Flatt Bridge

Once commonplace, more than 94 per cent of lowland raised bogs have disappeared in the last 150 years: dug for fuel, or more recently, sold as garden peat. At Langlands Moss, the part felling of a commercial conifer plantation, which had reduced the water table to dangerous levels, and the damming of old forest drainage channels has helped refill the pools and bring the moss back to life.

sundew

Langlands is easily reached from Calderglen via a prepared and sign-posted path alongside the River Calder and supports a specialised habitat of dragonflies, birds and some 28 species of plants, including cranberry and the carnivorous sundew. Hopefully it will be able to resist the steady expansion of the nearby industrial estate.

Walk to the end of the car park, passing the zoo and Calderglen Conservatory, turn left following signs to nature trails and the adventure play area, and pass through a red barrier. Go right and descend to the Rotten Calder opposite the Horseshoe Falls bridge. Don't cross over, but turn right and follow the woodland path alongside Torrance House Golf Club and mostly high above the river, before descending to the waterfalls of Flatt Linn.

Beyond these the path passes under the old (1791) and new (1999) Flatt

START & FINISH: *Calderglen Country Park car park (NS653527)*
DISTANCE: *8.5km; 5.25 miles*
TIME: *2hrs 50mins*

MAP: *OS 64*
TERRAIN: *Roads & paths; some waymarking*
GRADE: *Easy*

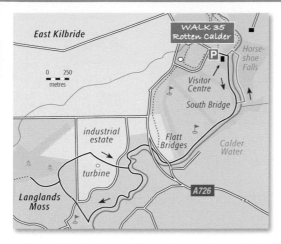

large wind turbine.

Follow the road right, then go left onto a path running down beside another golf course to the entrance to Langlands Moss. Follow the boardwalk out over Langlands Moss Local Nature Reserve, then back again to the main path. Turn left and follow the path round to meet Langlands Drive and go left then right back onto a path leading to the riverside path junction.

Bridge and the landscape changes from wooded river valley to meadow and open fields. Continue straight on where the path divides following the sign-posted riverside path to Langlands Moss and Auldhouse to emerge onto Langlands Drive along from the super-market depot and dominated by a single

Return by the outward route via the Flatt Bridges. If desired the South Bridge can be used near the end for a return along the right bank of the Rotten Calder before crossing back at the Horseshoe Falls bridge.

Access & Parking free

Langlands Moss

Beside The River Avon

Chatelherault West Lodge

Set on a hill among the Hamilton High Parks and built for the Duke of Hamilton as a summer residence, hunting lodge and dog kennels, Chatelherault is all that remains of a grandiose 18th century landscape design, in which a tree-lined Grand Avenue connected it with Hamilton Palace in the Low Parks, some two kilometres to the north-west.

The Duchy of Chatelherault was gifted to the Hamiltons, Earls of Arran, by the King of France for their part in organising the 1548 marriage of the Scottish Queen Mary to the French heir. The 11th and 12th Dukes of Hamilton are buried at Brodick Castle and their graves are passed on the walk to **Cnocan Gorge** [1].

The Industrial Revolution and coal-mining enriched the Hamiltons, as it did the Montgomeries at Eglinton Castle [**9**, **10. 11**], but it was also the undoing of Hamilton Palace; subsidence, the 'coal-miners' revenge', led to demolition of the mansion in 1928. The William Adam designed Chatelherault was not as badly affected – the walls of the West Lodge still show a distinct tilt – but the building was left to deteriorate and soon became a ruin.

Council acquisition in the 1970s was followed by restoration in the 1980s to near former glory and Chatelherault now forms the centrepiece of the Country Park which surrounds the deep wooded gorge of the Avon Water, known locally as the River Avon.

From the car park ascend to the rear of Chatelherault and enter the Visitor Centre from where the interior of the East Lodge can be explored. Return to the entrance, turn right and follow the internal path round the garden to exit at the side of the West Lodge overlooking

START & FINISH: *Chatelherault Country Park car park (NS738538)*
DISTANCE: *6km; 3.75 miles*
TIME: *2hrs*

MAP: *OS 64*
TERRAIN: *Waymarked paths*
GRADE: *Easy*

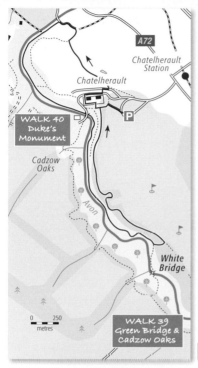

WALK 40
Duke's
Monument

Cadzow
Oaks

A72

Chatelherault
Station

Chatelherault

P

Avon

White
Bridge

0   250
metres

WALK 39
Green Bridge &
Cadzow Oaks

the remains of the Grand Avenue.

Go right along the drive then down steps and right along an access road to pick up the Deer Park Track and follow it left through pasture to enter the Grand Avenue, from where the route descends rightwards to a road. Go left here and down towards the Old Avon Bridge, then left through a walled entrance back into the park.

Follow the route of the old mineral railway beside the river, to steps below the arched Duke's Bridge which carries the road utilised by the Green Bridge & Cadzow Oaks [39] and Duke's Monument [40] walks over the Avon. Beyond the viaduct the route ascends to a higher path, then follows that back down to the river and more steps, beyond which the path divides.

The right-hand path leads to the White Bridge, closed at the time of writing by landslides. When open, the river can be crossed here to link with the path on the other side. Instead, turn left, climb the steps to the upper path and follow it back to Chatelherault.

Access & Parking free

Chatelherault East Lodge

101

Huntsman's Ride – Chatelherault

Green Bridge across the Avon

Dendrochronology, the method of ageing trees by counting their annual growth rings, is of little use for Chatelherault's ancient Cadzow Oaks; the oldest specimens are hollow. Some experts think they might be 600 years old, others 900.

Recently incorporated into the Clyde Valley Woodlands Nature Reserve, there are several hundred of these distinctively gnarled oaks at Chatelherault. Most can only be seen from a distance, but a small number can be admired up close.

Cadzow was granted to the Hamiltons in the 14th century by Robert I (The Bruce). The castle on the west bank of the Avon dates from the 16th century. Although largely destroyed during the turbulent lifetime of Mary (Queen of Scots), significant parts of the present structure were remodelled and landscaped in the 19th century.

From the car park ascend to the rear of Chatelherault and the Visitor Centre. This offers a range of displays exploring the rocks exposed in the deep gorge of the Avon, as well as access to the interior of the East Lodge.

Descend a path from outside the Visitor Centre to a road and follow it left across the Duke's Bridge over the Avon with views across to the ruins of Cadzow Castle. On the other side, keep left on the signposted path to the Cadzow Oaks.

After the oaks the trail continues

Cadzow Oak

START & FINISH: *Chatelherault Country Park car park (NS738538)*
DISTANCE: *8.5km; 5.25 miles*
TIME: *2hrs 50mins*
MAP: *OS 64*
TERRAIN: *Waymarked paths*
GRADE: *Easy*

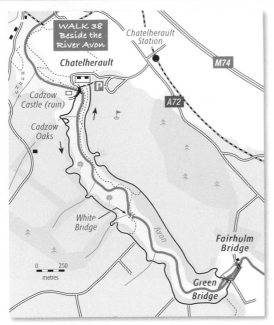

descends on the left to the White Bridge.

Continue south on the main path and descend to the Green Bridge. Just before the bridge a pleasant diversion can be had by going through the gate on the right then following the road towards Fairholm Bridge. Cross over then left and follow the riverside path back to the Green Bridge.

From there steep and sometimes muddy steps lead up to a good path high above the east bank of the Avon. This leads north and back to the Visitor Centre, meeting with the White Bridge trail en route and a possible extension onto the route

through forest and across numerous small burns and glens high above the west bank of the Avon. Shortly after the electricity pylons a brick-faced path

Beside The River Avon [38].

Access & Parking free

West side of the Avon

Barncluith

Old Avon Bridge at the northern end of the Country Park provides the link for this circular walk to the monument to William Duke of Hamilton in the north-west corner of the park. From the entrance to the Visitor Centre walk down left to a junction and go down the road and across the Duke's Bridge over the Avon. Turn right after the bridge and up a tarmac track past the ruins of Cadzow Castle to a T-junction. A path leads rightwards alongside the field, then into woodland becoming more of a track with occasional waymarks.

Keep left at a vague path junction to exit onto an access road leading left to High Parks Farm. It is worth walking up this road a short distance to the parkland, to view scattered remnants of the ancient Cadzow Oaks, some of which are thought to be 600 years old. Follow the road north, down towards Barncluith and the colonnaded circular monument in the woodland opposite.

Duke of Hamilton's Memorial

START & FINISH: *Chatelherault Country Park car park (NS738538)*
DISTANCE: *5.5km; 3.5 miles*
TIME: *1hr 50mins*

MAP: *OS 64*
TERRAIN: *Roads & paths; some waymarking, muddy in places*
GRADE: *Easy*

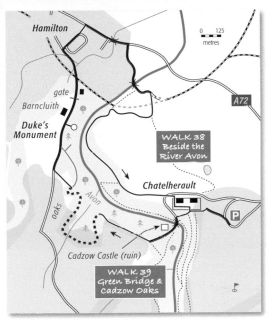

Hamilton

gate
Barncluith

Duke's Monument

0   125
metres

A72

WALK 38 Beside the River Avon

Chatelherault

P

oaks

Avon

Cadzow Castle (ruin)

WALK 39 Green Bridge & Cadzow Oaks

arched entrance on the right, but continue ahead on the road to a second entrance, from where signposts indicate the route back to the Visitor Centre and main buildings, which are soon seen straight ahead.

At the first path junction turn right and follow the Huntsman's Ride round into woodland above the Avon. Continue ahead at the main path junction to arrive at Chatelherault's West Lodge. Go through the gate in the front wall before the lodge and follow the path round the formal garden back to the Visitor Centre.

This commemorates the life of William Alexander, 11th Duke of Hamilton, who died in 1863 and is buried at Brodick Castle on the Isle of Arran, along with his son, the 12th Duke.

Continue on down the road through the blue gate – there is a pedestrian gate at the side if the main gate is closed – and on over the railway. Take the first right into Fergus Gardens and walk down to the end, from where an alley leads out to the main road. Go right here past Laverock Avenue and over a bridge across a burn, to Old Avon Road. Descend this to its end and cross over the 17th century Old Avon Bridge.

On the other side, don't go through the

Access & Parking free

Cadzow Castle

107

South Calder Water

Strathclyde Loch and the banks of the South Calder Water form a semi-rural landscape surrounded by urban development and traffic noise. Escaping the latter isn't easy, but this route makes the most of the surrounding woodland to screen out the worst. The cliff-lined glen of the South Calder is lush and pretty and crossed by the impressive Orbiston Viaduct. However, the close proximity to housing means litter can be a problem and the path on the east side of the river is avoided for that reason.

Start from the foreshore car park beyond M&D's Theme Park. Go down to the loch and turn left following the path round the shore to a junction. Keep left and follow the path straight up towards the road. Just before the road turn right and cross the bridge over the river, then right again to view the ruins of Bothwellhaugh Roman Baths which served the fort on the hill to the north.

Return back over the bridge to the road, cross it to a gravel path and follow that straight ahead through woodland to a junction in open parkland. Turn right following signs to Motherwell then right again past children's swings to the edge of Bellshill golf course and a junction at pillars: all that remains of Orbiston House.

The path on the right leads down to the South Calder Water. Continue left following the track to where it divides, then descend rightwards to the South Calder Water and continue below the sandstone crags above the river. The deep glen shields all traffic noise save for trains crossing the high stone arches of the Orbiston Viaduct above.

Pass the weir at the old Fairways mill and mill pond and through a more open section of river bank popular with anglers, then swing left and up to join the old road. Follow that left to a signpost and tarmac path leading uphill

START & FINISH: *Strathclyde Country Park, Foreshore car park (NS726579)*

DISTANCE: *6.5km; 4 miles*

TIME: *2hrs 10mins*

MAP: *OS 64*

TERRAIN: *Roads, tracks & paths*

GRADE: *Easy*

over grass to a residential area and signposted Strathclyde Park. Turn left past Bellshill Golf Course club house to railings and an entrance signposted for Strathclyde Country Park.

The gravel track leads down through woodland dividing the golf course, crosses over the railway and joins the outward route. Follow this back past the Orbiston pillars to the junction beyond the children's swings. Veer right here and cross over Bothwellhaugh Road and through a car park into Bothwellhaugh Plantation.

Go left at the first obvious turning and descend steadily through the forest on a wide path to a four-way junction. Cross slightly left, then straight ahead and over a bridge. Continue straight ahead at the three-way junction just after this, to emerge at the toilets opposite the foreshore car park.

Access & Parking free

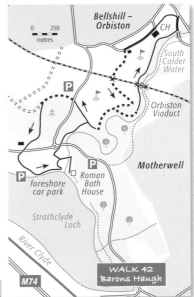

WALK 42
Barons Haugh

Old bridge in Strathclyde park

Barons Haugh

Barons Haugh RSPB Nature Reserve

Dalzell Estate and Barons Haugh RSPB Nature Reserve lie to the south-east of Strathclyde Loch but are easily reached from the Country Park by a pleasant ramble along the Clyde Walkway. Historic Dalzell House is centred round a 16th century keep which has been extended and altered through the centuries, although the original building can still be clearly identified. James Hamilton bought the land from the Dalzells in 1647 and Hamiltons lived there until 1952 when the estate was sold to the local council and the house subsequently divided into flats.

From the Beach car park at the southern end of Strathclyde Loch follow the lochside path to the road and cross directly over into Clyde Park. Follow the tarmac cycle path below the red iron bridge carrying the A723 over the river and ascend to houses.

Go round these, then rightwards back into woodland and on past the cemetery and below the railway viaduct. After a turning on the left the path divides. Keep right alongside the river following the path past two bird hides on the flooded meadows of Barons Haugh. Go past a path off left up the Chestnut Walk beside the Dalzell Burn and on through an avenue of lime trees to where the path divides, and swing left into Adders Gill Wood.

Ascend through the woodland keeping ahead at the next junction to a T-junction. Turn left and follow the path through enclosed woodland with a diversion right to the 'Listening Cave' and a view of the house. Back on the main path, continue past a track off to the right over the river, then drop down and cross a small stone footbridge over the Dalzell Burn to a railinged mausoleum and cemetery.

START & FINISH: *Strathclyde Country Park, Beach car park (NS726579)*

DISTANCE: *12km; 7.5 miles*

TIME: *4hrs*

MAP: *OS 64*

TERRAIN: *Tracks & paths*

GRADE: *Easy / Moderate*

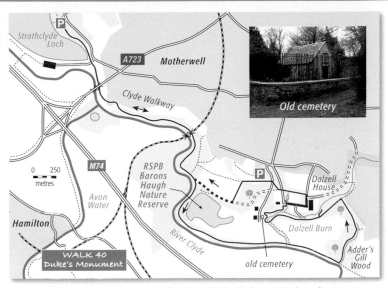

Strathclyde Loch

A723 Motherwell

Clyde Walkway

Old cemetery

M74

0 250
metres

Avon Water

Hamilton

RSPB Barons Haugh Nature Reserve

P

Dalzell House

River Clyde

old cemetery

Dalzell Burn

Adder's Gill Wood

WALK 40 Duke's Monument

Follow the path clockwise round the mausoleum then along the left side of the burn passing St Patrick's Well and a stone gazebo above the path known as Lord Gavin's Temple. Continue on the path by the burn to the larger Sow Bridge and exit left to the access road

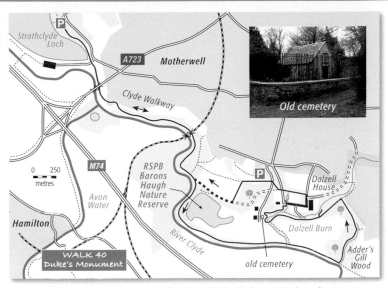

Railway viaduct over the Clyde

to Dalzell House. Explore the Japanese Garden opposite then follow the road towards the house, passing an oak allegedly planted by David I (1124-53) and called the Covenanter's Oak after the outdoor services held in its shelter during the religious violence which followed the restoration of Charles II.

Continue left past the house, then left onto a path which crosses the top of the Japanese Garden to an access road. Cross over this then turn right to meet the main access road opposite the car park. Go through the car park onto a path which leads through open land before turning down left to join a track. Turn right and follow the track along the top end of Barons Haugh back to the Clyde Walkway and retrace your steps to the start.

Access & Parking free

Monkland Canal

While much of the Forth and Clyde and Union canals escaped the motorways and urban development of the past 60 years, the Monkland Canal has not. Of the original 12 miles less than half still exists and this walk links the extensive path network surrounding Drumpellier's lochs, parkland and woods, with the remaining western section.

From the car park beyond the Visitor Centre follow the path over the small bridge and round the eastern side of Lochend Loch. Leave the tarmac lochside path for a tarmac track signposted 'Playingfields Loop', then leave that for a gravel path on the left which brings you onto the nursery access road. Turn left then right onto another path heading into woodland and follow it to a metal kissing gate.

Go through this, over the railway bridge and left onto a track, then straight on beside the railway to emerge on the park access road and open grassland beside the Monkland Canal. Surveyed and partially engineered by James Watt, the canal opened in 1790, principally to transport coal from the Lanarkshire fields to Glasgow, and closed in 1935.

Follow the canal bank, then the access road to exit onto Blair Road. Turn right, down Blair Road and over the canal to gain the towpath, and follow this back towards Drumpellier. A short distance along it is possible to descend left to a track in the woods which regains the towpath further on. Where the towpath divides keep right under the bridge and continue along the canal beside the golf course, until the path turns left and descends to housing.

Although urban development, roads and railways have chopped the canal into separate sections, the water is far from stagnant and lifeless as the occasional heron shows. Return to the

START & FINISH: *Drumpellier Country Park car park (NS705664)*

DISTANCE: *7.5km; 2.5 miles*

TIME: *2hrs 30mins*

MAP: *OS 64*

TERRAIN: *Tracks & paths; some waymarks, muddy in places*

GRADE: *Easy*

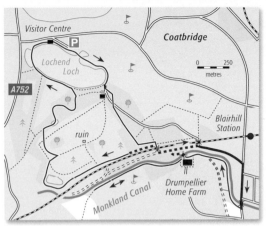

Home Farm Wood, to join a gravel path. Continue ahead on a grassy path then swing round the left side of a large pond to a hedge. Pass through and follow it right to join the gravel path. Turn left, ascend to a high point by the round Gilmourneuk Wood, then down to a stile.

A right turn leads through woodland and over boardwalks through a marshy area to arrive on a straight bridge, ascend the steps, cross back over section with the nursery visible at its the canal and follow the track back over end. Turn left to gain Lochend Loch the railway to the metal kissing gate. then left again and follow the tarmac

Do not go through, but turn immedi- path round and across the causeway ately left onto a grassy track running back to the Visitor Centre and car park. parallel to the railway and follow it out into the new plantation of Drumpellier

Access & Parking free

Lochend Loch

Stirling & Dunbartonshire

Gartmorn Dam &
the Ochils

*A*way from the big cities, the Country Parks in this chapter are located in a more rural landscape, although it's hard to completely escape Central Scotland's industrial heritage and the needs of its urban population.

Many of the parks feature castles and stately homes, built and later abandoned by wealthy bankers and industrialists. Balloch Castle on the southern shore of Loch Lomond is one of the best preserved of these. The extensive grounds and lochside gardens are easily explored via the **Fairy Glen & The Castle [44]**, while the nearby Woodland Trust Scotland reserve at **Knockour & Whinny Hill**

[45] offers a more extended route with elevated views over the loch and surrounding hills.

Further east, on the high ground immediately north of Glasgow, lies Mugdock Country Park. This park offers a range of walks and links to an extensive network of rural paths including the West Highland Way. **Mugdock's Castles [46]** lie at the heart of the park and are easily visited via a short walk suitable for families. Anyone wanting a longer outing can explore **Craigallion & Mugdock Wood [47]** to the north and the Milngavie reservoirs to the south which have been **Delivering Glasgow's Water [48]** for more than 150 years.

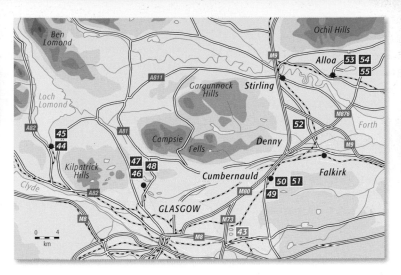

Palacerigg Country Park near Cumbernauld has a fascinating history. Purchased in 1900 by Glasgow's Distress Committee, the farm offered labour to the city's unemployed right up to the 1940s. The peat land surrounding **Fannyside Loch [49]** and **Toddle Moor [50]** was heavily worked and generated income for the farm and its labourers. A more extensive route links the park's paths with **Glencryan Woods [51]** and the Scottish Wildlife Trust reserve of Forest Wood.

Plean's Black Gold [52] highlights the coal industry which once dominated Central Scotland and can be

BALLOCH CASTLE COUNTRY PARK

Located at Balloch at the southern end of Loch Lomond

West Dunbartonshire Council
<www.west-dunbarton.gov.uk>

Loch Lomond & The Trossachs National Park
<www.lochlomond-trossachs.org>

Getting There
Foot: *From Balloch*

Road: *From Glasgow & Edinburgh –* *M8, A82. From Stirling – A811, A82*

Train: *Balloch (1.5km to Balloch Castle), First ScotRail see p7*

Bus: *See p7*

Facilities
Visitor Centre: *Balloch Castle, toilets*

Countryside Ranger Service: *Walks & educational events*

Other Activities: *Play area*

Further Information
Woodland Trust Scotland:

MUGDOCK COUNTRY PARK

Located on the outskirts of Milngavie, north of Glasgow

East Dunbartonshire Council
<www.eastdunbarton.gov.uk>

Stirling Council
<www.stirling.gov.uk>

Getting There
Foot: From Milngavie via the West Highland Way

Road: From Glasgow – A81. From Edinburgh – M8, A81. From Stirling – A811, A81

Train: Milngavie (3km), FirstScotRail see p7

Bus: See p7

Facilities
Craigend Visitor Centre: (0141 9566100), toilets

Countryside Ranger Service: Walks & educational events

Other Activities: Children's play area, orienteering courses

Food, Drink & Shops: Visitor Centre cafe, restaurant, farm shop, BBQs (hire), gifts, arts & crafts, garden centre

Further Information
Mugdock Country Park:
<www.mugdock-country-park.org.uk>

PALACERIGG COUNTRY PARK

Located at Cumbernauld

North Lanarkshire Council
<www.northlanarkshire.gov.uk>

Getting There
Foot: From Cumbernauld

Road: From Glasgow – M8, M80, A8011, B8054. From Edinburgh – M8, M73, M80, A8011, B8054. From Stirling – M80, A8011, B8054

Train: Cumbernauld (800m), FirstScotRail see p7

Bus: See 7

Facilities
Visitor Centre: (01236 720047), toilets

Countryside Ranger Service: Walks & educational events

Other Activities: Rare breeds centre, children's play area, golf course

Food & Drink: Visitor Centre cafe

Further Information
Rare Breeds Survival Trust:
<www.rbst.org.uk>

Scottish Wildlife Trust:
<www.swt.org.uk>

PLEAN COUNTRY PARK

Located at Plean, south of Stirling

Stirling Council
<www.stirling.gov.uk>

Getting There
Foot: From Plean

Road: From Glasgow – M80, A91, A9
From Edinburgh – M9, A91, A9
From Stirling – A9

Bus: See p7

Facilities
Car Park: Toilets

Countryside Ranger Service: Walks & educational events

Palacerigg Country Park

seen all over this Country Park, from the landscaped bings to the commemorative statue in the car park.

Coal mining also led to the building of Gartmorn Dam, the location for the last walks in this chapter. Once the largest artificial expanse of water in Scotland, Gartmorn started life as a ready supply for the waterwheel

driving the pumps in the Earl of Mar's surrounding coal mines, before becoming a water supply for the local area and ending as a Local Nature Reserve. A walk **Around Gartmorn Loch [53]** is suitable for most abilities, while the walks to **Gartmorn Hill [54]** and **Fairy Gartmorn to Hillend [55]** link the park to the wider path network.

GARTMORN DAM COUNTRY PARK

Located at Alloa

Clackmannanshire Council
<www.clacksweb.gov.uk>

Getting There
Foot: *From Alloa*

Road: *From Glasgow – M8, M80, A91, A907, A908. From Edinburgh – M9, M876, A876, A907, A908. From Stirling – A91, A907, A908*

Train: *Alloa (3km), FirstScotRail see p7*

Bus: *See p7*

Facilities
Visitor Centre: *Toilets*

Countryside Ranger Service: *Walks & educational events*

Other Activities: *Bird watching, fishing*

Further Information
Forestry Commission Scotland:

Balloch Castle

Balloch Castle and its 200 acres of parkland lie on the southern banks of Loch Lomond and are easily reached by train, bus or car from Balloch Road in the heart of the town.

Built in 1808 for banker John Buchanan, the mock-castle and estate were bought by Glasgow Corporation in the 1900s and became a Country Park in the 1980s. Now run by West Dunbartonshire Council, the park lies within the Loch Lomond and The Trossachs National Park and has bene-fitted from new signage and improved footpaths in recent years.

The best starting point is the Moss o' Balloch car park on the north side of the bridge over the River Leven. From the car park follow the wall east beside the main Balloch Road to gain the South Gate access road. Follow this towards the castle and pass round to its front for fine views across the parkland to the loch.

Continue past the Chinese Garden on a tarmac path to where the route to **Knockour & Whinny Hill [45]** branches off right, and descend through wood-land to just after a bench on the right. Here a smaller path is followed off right to the Burn of Balloch and the Fairy Glen, before rejoining the main path.

The route then continues on the

START & FINISH: *Moss o' Balloch car park, Balloch Road (NS 392820)*
DISTANCE: *5km; 3 miles*
TIME: *1hr 40mins*
MAP: *OS 57*
TERRAIN: *Waymarked paths*
GRADE: *Easy*

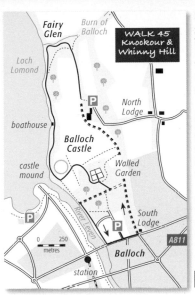

**WALK 45
Knockour &
Whinny Hill**

lochside passing an adventure play-ground and a boathouse, to arrive at the mouth of the River Leven. On the left is the site of the old castle built by the Earls of Lennox, although little remains save for the raised foundations and a long-dry moat.

Soon after this, a yellow-waymarked path is followed off left across the park-land below the house. Keep following the waymarks rightwards into the woodland to gain prepared paths which lead round to the arched entrance into the old Walled Garden.

After exploring this, exit the garden straight ahead to a rough track and follow it down right to a junction with the path beside the River Leven. Go left here and follow the riverside path to the main road. A left turn leads back to the car park.

Access & Parking free

Entrance to the Walled Garden

Ascending Whinny Hill

According to the Wikipedia website it appears there are no less than 10 hills named Mount Misery in the USA, in addition to one in Canada, one in the Falklands and one on the island of Saint Kitts in the Caribbean. Although there are none listed for Scotland, Mount Misery is clearly marked on Bartholomew maps from the late 1940s at the south end of Loch Lomond.

Exactly why the hill was Mount Misery isn't known, but today it is known as Knockour Hill and with Whinny Hill to its south, it makes up the Woodland Trust Scotland reserve of Whinny Hill Wood. Since the wood came into the trust's care in 1997, it has steadily been removing many of the commercially planted conifers and replacing them with native species.

The wood is easily reached from the North Lodge car park of Balloch Castle Country Park, signposted and accessed from Mollanbowie Road at the eastern edge of Balloch. Gain the tarmac path on the far side of the car park and follow it north through open parkland. Just as you enter woodland a gravel path branches off right, contours round to the Burn of Balloch, then ascends to the private access road to Boturich Castle.

Cross over into Whinny Hill Wood and ascend straight ahead through a mixture of established broadleaf woodland and new planting to gain an old boundary wall. This section may be muddy in places, although the worst bits can be avoided with care. The path then levels out before dropping down again to a new gate and fencing, which can also be wet and muddy.

Keep right, then left here to another gate, then descend through another cleared area with new planting to a junction with a track.

START & FINISH: *Balloch Castle, North Lodge car park (NS 391830)*

DISTANCE: *9km; 5.5 miles*

TIME: *3hrs*

MAP: *OS 57*

TERRAIN: *Roads, tracks & paths; muddy in places*

GRADE: *Easy / Moderate*

Follow the track leftwards, then right through a gate to a gated deer fence, from where a path ascends through another newly planted area to conifer woodland surrounding the hill top. Pass through the conifers and out the other side, again muddy in places, and continue ascending to the summit clearing with a bench and views over Loch Lomond to the Luss Hills.

Continue on the path which descends out of the woodland and through the deer fence back to the track. From here it is possible to return by the outward route, but a more inter-esting, if longer alternative is to turn left and follow the track to a T-junction with a forest road.

Follow the forest road left with fine views across to Conic Hill and Ben Lomond, before descending to Lorn farm and on to the turning to Boturich Castle where the track becomes a tarmac access road. Follow this back to the path into the Country Park along-side the Burn of Balloch.

Access & Parking free

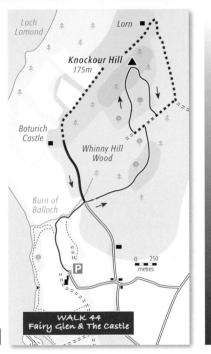

WALK 44
Fairy Glen & The Castle

Approaching Lorn

Below Knockour Hill

Mugdock Castle

Situated on a ridge of high ground between Glasgow and Strath Blane, Mugdock offers a network of waymarked routes in addition to easy access to the surrounding countryside via the West Highland Way and other established tracks and paths.

Mugdock's elevation gives it fine views north to Ben Lomond, Dumgoyne and the Campsie Fells and south over Glasgow. This was particularly useful during WWII when anti-aircraft gun emplacements were established on the western flanks of the park and these can be explored during the walk. However, the main points of interest in the park are its two very different castles – Craigend and Mugdock.

From the Visitor Centre follow the main path south towards Craigend Castle. This isn't a castle as such but a ruined mansion and was built in the early 1800s for Glasgow merchants and politicians, the Smiths. John Smith & Sons booksellers started in 1751, managed to weather the upheaval in bookselling and continues as a major retail outlet in universities. In the early 1900s the castle was tenanted by George Outram, owner of The *Glasgow Herald* newspaper, and subsequently operated as a zoo until 1956.

Turn right beyond the castle onto a path signposted to the Khyber car park and from there, follow the track left to Mugdock Castle, passing the old gun emplacements on the right. These can be explored and interpretation boards explain how they worked and the jobs of the troops who manned them.

Mugdock Castle lies in a commanding

START & FINISH: *Mugdock Country Park car park (NS 537783)*

DISTANCE: *4.5km; 2.75 miles*

TIME: *1hr 30mins*

MAP: *OS 64*

TERRAIN: *Waymarked tracks & paths; some signposts*

GRADE: *Easy*

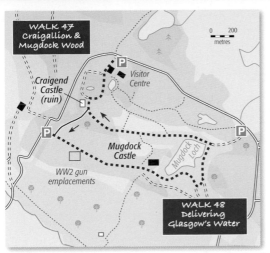

WALK 47
Craigallion & Mugdock Wood

Craigend Castle (ruin)

Visitor Centre

Mugdock Castle

Mugdock Loch

WW2 gun emplacements

WALK 48
Delivering Glasgow's Water

0   200
metres

Earl of Montrose, in the 1600s, the castle retains a small but significant place in Scottish history. Most of the castle is in ruins, save for the south-west tower which has been restored.

Continue past the castle on a track which leads round the southern end of Mugdock Loch to a junction. Turn left here and follow the wide path round the east end of the loch to another T-junction.

position, guarding the northern approaches to Glasgow and dates from the 1300s. A power centre for the Grahams during the Wars of Independence and for James Graham,

Take a further left and follow the main path back to Craigend Castle and the Visitor Centre.

Access & Parking free

Craigend Castle

Carbeth Loch & Dumgoyne

In the 1930s Craigallion became a rural retreat from unemployment and overcrowding in the city. The focus was a fire, fed by wood from the surrounding forest, and around which anyone could gather.

During the war years the steady stream of weekend walkers and climbers started to move on from Craigallion to explore The Cobbler, Glen Coe and Ben Nevis. By the mid-1950s walking and climbing in the Highlands was no longer the sole preserve of the well-off.

The Fire at Craigallion survived largely thanks to landowner Allen Barns-Graham and the period is well captured in *Creag Dhu Climber*, Jeff Connor's biography of Glasgow climber John Cunningham. Barns-Graham also established the huts beside Carbeth Loch at the northern end of the walk.

From the large car park at Mugdock Country Park, pass to the right of the Visitor Centre and follow a wide sign-posted path round to the right. Stick to the main path as it descends and, as the ruins of Craigend Castle come in sight, go right over a boardwalk across a burn and ascend to a gap in the wall beside the road.

Cross over, turn left and descend the road to a wooden gate and signpost indicating a Public Footpath to the B821 and Cuilt Brae. Follow the sign-posted track through the forest, passing overhead pylon wires to reach a junction with a track on the left. If you arrive at a metal gate you have over-shot your turning.

Turn left and follow the rough track down through the forest to views over the huts and Carbeth Loch. Go over a stile and turn sharp left onto another track which is part of the West Highland Way (WHW). This leads past the loch and huts to a junction with a Public Footpath sign to Cuilt Brae. It is

START & FINISH: *Mugdock Country Park car park (NS 537783)*

DISTANCE: *9km; 5.5 miles*

TIME: *3hrs*

MAP: *OS 64*

TERRAIN: *Tracks & paths; some waymarking, muddy in places*

GRADE: *Easy / Moderate*

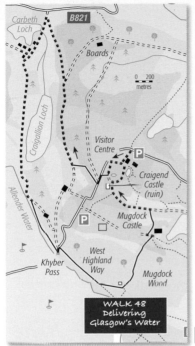

worth taking this path for a short distance for a fine view over Carbeth Loch to Dumgoyne and Slackdhu. Return to the main route and continue to Craigallion Loch, passing back under the pylon wires to meet the Allander Water and arrive at the road near the so-called Khyber Pass. Follow the road for a short distance left, then turn right back onto the WHW and through the bluebell-carpeted Mugdock Wood.

At the first junction turn left off the WHW following signs to Mugdock Castle and the Visitor Centre. Go through a walled twist in the path to arrive at the castle, one-time seat of the Grahams and James, Marquis of Montrose.

From here, follow the Visitor Centre signs left of the castle to a boardwalk and a main track which leads left past the ruins of Craigend Castle, built in the 1800s for Glasgow merchants and booksellers the Smiths. Turn right at the junction beyond and skirt the small loch back to the Visitor Centre.

Access & Parking free

Carbeth Loch

Mugdock Country Park & local paths
Delivering Glasgow's Water

Mugdock Reservoir

Built by Glasgow Corporation Waterworks as part of the Loch Katrine water scheme, Mugdock and Craigmaddie reservoirs provided drinking water direct to the city for more than 150 years.

Both reservoirs still perform this function, although supplies now pass through Scottish Water's state-of-the-art water treatment plant, which was opened in 2008 at a cost of £110m.

Situated at the south-eastern boundary of the Country Park, the reservoirs are easily combined with the area's wider path network. From the Visitor Centre car park follow the signposted path round to the ruined Craigend Castle, from where a path leads right, signposted to Khyber car park.

From there a track leads east to Mugdock Castle, passing old gun emplacements, built in 1941 following the Clydebank blitz. These can be explored and interpretation boards explain their role and the jobs of the troops manning them.

Continue to a path junction outside the main entrance to the castle; the route turns right at this junction but it is worth exploring the 14th century castle first.

Exit straight ahead from the castle, signposted to the West Highland Way and Mugdock Wood, and follow the path to where it divides. Go right and down through the fine broadleaf woodland of Mugdock Wood and a wall sculpture to sections of boardwalk.

Continue past a ruined building to a junction signposted right to Khyber Pass and on to a main junction with the West Highland Way. Turn left to Milngavie and Drumclog Moor and follow the Allander Water beside Milngavie golf course to a four-way junction. Go left here ascending onto Drumclog Moor to join a main path and follow it right to Drumclog car park on the minor road beside Mugdock Reservoir.

This was the first reservoir built for John La Trobe Bateman's ambitious 1859 project which transported water via aqueduct from Loch Katrine, 26 miles away. Increasing water demand led to the building of Craigmaddie,

START & FINISH: *Mugdock Country Park car park (NS 537783)*
DISTANCE: *9km; 5.5 miles*
TIME: *3hrs*

MAP: *OS 64*
TERRAIN: *Roads, tracks & paths; some signposts & waymarks*
GRADE: *Easy / Moderate*

which was completed in 1896 and supplied by a second aqueduct.

Cross the road to the tarmac path beside Mugdock Reservoir and follow it anti clockwise, with southerly views at the dam end over Milngavie and Tannoch Loch to Glasgow. Continue around Craigmaddie (or cross the causeway between the two reservoirs) and follow the water-edge walkway through woodland to the bridge at the northern end of Mugdock Reservoir.

Cross the bridge, exit to the road and turn right, following the pavement north. Where the pavement ends a short section of road needs care before a path on the left leads into woodland

and beside the burn in a pleasant small gorge. Continue past the South Lodge car park to a path junction. Go right and on to another junction, then right again to the Visitor Centre – the left turn is to Mugdock Castle.

At the T-junction, turn left beside Mugdock Loch with views across to Mugdock Castle. Just past a small cliff on the path and the end of the loch, a path on the right leads up to parkland and views of ruined Craigend Castle. A right at the next junction skirts the right side of the Craigend Pond below the walled garden and the car park.

Access & Parking free

129

Palacerigg Visitor Centre

Palacerigg offers a variety of routes on paths and tracks, the most accessible of which are followed by this circular route to Fannyside Loch and back.

The Country Park encompasses most of the old Palacerigg Farm, bought by Glasgow's Distress Committee in the early 1900s and used as a farm colony, offering work to the city's unemployed. Only married men with children and good references got work, but in return for their labour they received food, lodgings and return rail fare to Glasgow, a further 8s per week going to their wives and 1s 6d to each child.

Most of the work involved growing vegetables and peat cutting, both of which were sold through city markets. More than 90 acres of moorland were reclaimed for cultivation and much of the central area of the old farm is now covered by Palacerigg Golf Course.

Glasgow Corporation took over on the abolition of the Distress Committee

in 1930, and Palacerigg continued to provide work during the Great Depression and up to WWII. The farm became a Country Park in the mid-1970s but continues its agricultural traditions as a rare breeds centre assisting in the conservation of Eriskay ponies, North Ronaldsay and Boreray sheep, Shetland and White Park cattle and Scots grey poultry. Information

START & FINISH: *Palacerigg Country Park car park (NS 787733)*
DISTANCE: *4.5 km; 2.75 miles*
TIME: *1hr 30mins*

MAP: *OS 64*
TERRAIN: *Waymarked tracks*
GRADE: *Easy*

boards indicate where these animals can be found in the surrounding fields and the children's farm near the Visitor Centre.

From the car park walk back along the access road and turn left onto a gated track signposted to Laverock Trail, Treetop Way and Fallow Deer. Down on the left, the raised treetop walkway gives a pleasant diversion with views south-west to Goatfell on the Island of Arran. When the walkway ends, go down right to return to the track which leads up past farm buildings.

Continue on the track, passing a turning on the right to the Laverock Nature Trail taken by the route across **Toddle Moor** [50] and fields with sheep and ponies, to reach a T-junction facing Fannyside Loch. The lochside is easily reached from here via grass paths.

Return to the main track, which swings round left by the golf course to a junction. Turn right and continue beside the golf course to another T-junction. Take a left here and continue on the main track past Limekilns Pond and a signpost pointing right to Forest Woods and Abronhill, the route to **Glencryan Woods** [51].

At the next junction a path goes off right to Glencryan, but remain on the main track as it swings round left and follow it down past the archery area to meet the service road. This leads left to the children's play area and access into the children's farm which can be explored en route to the Visitor Centre and the walkway across the pond, back to the car park.

Access & Parking free

Treetop Walkway

Toddle Moor

The extraction of peat was big business at the start of the 20th century and Palacerigg farm colony had more than enough to go around. As part of Glasgow's Distress Committee's project providing work for the city's unemployed, workers would stream into Palacerigg every day to maintain the farm infrastructure, plant and harvest vegetables and dig peat. The main peat digging areas of Fannyside Moor and Toddle Moor, north and south of Fannyside Loch, were served by a specially built narrow-gauge railway which transported the farm's produce to a branch line and the city markets. As a sideline, a factory was set up producing firelighters from strips of peat dipped in flammable liquid.

From the car park walk back along the access road and turn left onto a gated track signposted to Laverock Trail, Treetop Way and Fallow Deer. On route a diversion can be made onto the raised treetop walkway on the left, for views south-west to Goatfell on the Island of Arran, before dropping down right to the track.

Beyond the farm buildings there are two options for accessing Toddle Moor. At a left-hand bend a path on the right signposted Laverock Trail starts in a forest break with overhead lines, then enters the forest. It's a pleasant path but can be wet and muddy in places. A drier option is to turn right before the signpost onto an obvious path beside the fence enclosing the field behind the buildings and follow this round, keeping a sharp eye out for the Laverock Trail which joins from the left and crosses over at waymarks.

Follow the Laverock Trail down across open ground and over a wooden footbridge, then ascend left of a fenced enclosure to a vehicle track, signposted right to Toddle Moor Trail and Picnic Site. Continue to an access gate, from where a fence leads down left to a

START & FINISH: *Palacerigg Country Park car park (NS 787733)*
DISTANCE: *5km; 3 miles*
TIME: *1hr 40mins*

MAP: *OS 64*
TERRAIN: *Waymarked tracks & paths; muddy in places*
GRADE: *Easy / Moderate*

WALK 51
Glencryan Woods

Forest Wood Wildlife Reserve SWT

Limekilns Pond

Fannyside Moor

WALK 49
Fannyside Loch

Visitor Centre

P CH

treetop walkway

Toddle Moor

0   250
metres

clear path which crosses the heather peat moorland and scattered silver birch via various wooden footbridges to a vehicle track lined with conifers.

Peat production stopped at WWII and didn't resume, but the herring bone pattern of the peat digging is clearly seen on Google Earth, if harder to make out on the ground! Turn left onto the vehicle track, the line of the old peat railway which followed the park's southern boundary, and follow it north

to Fannyside Loch. Remain on the track which swings left past a junction and across a fairway and two tees on the golf course. Signs warn you to beware of golf balls and golfers from right or left depending on direction of play. At the woodland strip turn right onto a path through an avenue of trees between fairways – the Lint Coble Nature Trail. Descend through pleasant broadleaf woodland past large ponds to more open ground and the continuation of the circular track. Turn left and follow the track round the golf course past the entrance to **Glencryan Woods** [51], and on to gain the service road. Continue straight over here onto a path leading down to the main access road which leads past the children's farm to the Visitor Centre and car park.

| Access & Parking free |

Fannyside Loch

Glencryan Woods

At the height of Palacerigg's time as a farm colony more than 800 men made the daily walk from Cumbernauld station, through Glencryan Woods at the north-west corner of the park, to their work on the farm.

This route combines recently upgraded paths and tracks through this woodland with the Country Park's more established path network and links them to tracks through the Scottish Wildlife Trust's Forest Wood reserve to the park's north-east.

The result is a diverse and interesting mixture of landscapes from the mown lawns of the golf course and mature deciduous woodland surrounding the deep ravine of the Glencryan Burn, to abandoned fireclay mines and the high rise flats of Cumbernauld .

From the car park, with the pond and visitor centre to your left, walk straight ahead on a signposted track leading out across the golf course. There should be no problems with golfers as you cross the initial short open section to the trees, but keep a good eye out nonetheless. Continue through the trees to posts on the left marking the start of a path, the Lint Cobble Nature Trail, through the woodland strip between the fairways.

The next section is common to the **Toddle Moor [50]** route and leads through broadleaf woodland and ponds to reach the outer track. Turn left here, then right shortly afterwards by the

START & FINISH: *Palacerigg Country Park car park (NS 787733)*

DISTANCE: *6.5km; 4 miles*

TIME: *2hrs 10mins*

MAP: *OS 64*

TERRAIN: *Tracks & paths; some signposting*

GRADE: *Easy / Moderate*

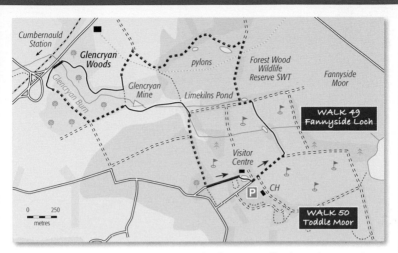

Limekilns Pond, signposted Forest Woods and Abronhill.

The track exits the Country Park into the SWT reserve and is followed across open ground and below pylons to a junction. Turn left here (the main track continues into broadleaf woodland) and follow the track round past a pond on the left and into broadleaf woodland with views past Cumbernauld's high flats to the Kilsyth Hills.

Exit the woodland and follow the track down and round towards Cumbernauld and a junction. Go left, pass below pylons and back into the Country Park at the woodland. Turn right just before the Glencryan Burn which crosses the track at the lowest point and follow the path above the deeply cut gorge and waterfall below. The path divides at one point but both routes lead down to the main road.

At the bottom go left and across the bottom of the gorge, then follow the path over the grass embankment and back into woodland. Continue to a four-way junction and turn left onto a path through woodland which ends with a steep descent to a point just up from the Glencryan Burn. Turn right and a short distance up on the left is the barred entrance to the Glencryan Fireclay Mine.

Turn right when the path joins the main orbital track and follow it to the service road. This is then followed left to the Visitor Centre and farm and pond walkway leading to the car park.

Access & Parking free

Footbridge over Plean Burn

Plean's landscape has been shaped by heavy industry, as witnessed by a statue of a helmeted miner in the main car park, 'dedicated to the coal miners who worked and died in the Plean pits'.

Plean House appears to have been built in the late 1700s by one William Simpson, a wealthy East India trader, though the past relationship between house, owner and pits is unclear. The last pits in the village closed in the early '60s and like the bings at either end of the Country Park, the house and stable block are slowly returning to nature.

The bings and coal mining detritus do mean that the park is surprisingly hilly considering its position on the flood plain of the River Forth. The hills aren't steep enough to increase your heart rate, but they are sufficient to maintain interest in the landscape.

From the car park left of the walled garden, continue past the toilet block following a tarmac path down to signposts and keep right, following coloured waymarks. Keep right at the next junction and pass over various footbridges to reach the Plean Burn. Cross over a path (this leads left towards the ruins of the old stables) and head right to follow the right-hand side of a wall through woodland to emerge near the ruins of the Greenkeeper's Cottage on the track rising from the old stables.

Follow this rightwards to the main track, turn right then immediately left over a small footbridge onto a path which ascends to the top of the whale-backed South Bing. This consists of shale and coal debris, colonised by silver birch and has fine views north to the Ochils. Continue round to join a horse-riding trail which comes in from the right and follow this to a junction. The horse trail goes right, but continue straight ahead to arrive back at the main track, a little bit along from the ruined cottage.

START & FINISH: *Plean Country Park car park (NS 827868)*
DISTANCE: *4km; 2.5 miles*
TIME: *1hr 20mins*

MAP: *OS 57*
TERRAIN: *Tracks & paths; some waymarking, muddy in places*
GRADE: *Easy / Moderate*

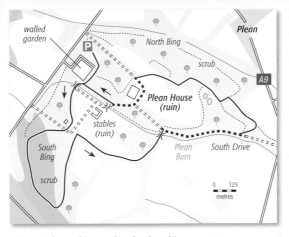

the valley on a rough path to gain the edge of the open parkland overlooking the ruins of Plean House.

Go through a wooden gate, turn right and follow the edge of the woodland to its end, where it starts to curve back right. From here head diagonally left to pick up a waymarked route and follow it down to the tarmac paths surrounding the ruined house, behind which is a picnic area, children's trail and wildlife pond.

A tarmac path leads around the front of the ruined house towards the old stables and the Plean Burn, from where a signpost indicates the route back alongside the right bank of the burn to the walled garden and car park.

Turn right and immediately ahead is a gate. Walk towards this then left onto a track, the extension of the horse trail left earlier. Go left, then right and through a wall, following a well-worn waymarked path running alongside a wall. The path leads through conifer woodland then descends through areas of new planting to cross over the Plean Burn at small bridge and meet the South Drive.

Descend the rhododendron-lined drive rightwards beside the Plean Burn to a bench and waymark pointing up left off the main track. Ascend the path, but ignore the waymarked path going off left which turns muddy very quickly, instead continuing straight ahead to reach the horse trail beside a fence, just beyond.

Follow the horse trail left to a junction, continuing left and down, then right onto a path leading past the ponds in the small wooded valley below. Leave this path for a waymarked route on the left which rises up out of

Access & Parking free

Gartmorn Loch

*A*t one time the largest artificial area of water in Scotland, the origins of Gartmorn Dam date back to the early days of the Industrial Revolution. Low-lying ground and close proximity to the Firth of Forth meant flooding was always a risk in the surrounding coal mines owned by the Earl of Mar.

Pumps could keep the problem at bay, but power was needed to work them and the principal power supply in the early 18th century was the waterwheel. That needed significantly more water than the local burns could provide.

The solution the Earl's English engineer George Sorocold, came up with was to build a horseshoe-shaped weir (now a B-listed 'building') at Forest Mill on the Black Devon river and dig a lade west to Gartmorn. A large earth dam at the eastern end retained the water, making Gartmorn Dam ready to supply the quantities required to power the Earl's machinery. In the immediate area, industry flourished as collieries and mills took advantage of the increased water flow.

As water power gave way to steam, Gartmorn Dam became increasingly important as a ready made supply of drinking water for the area's growing population. The Alloa Water Act of 1891 saw the loch enlarged and a pump house built to supply water to filter beds at the western end of the loch.

Although no longer used to supply water, Gartmorn is still owned by Scottish Water and leased to Clackmannanshire Council. The loch is a local nature reserve and a haven for birds, including a variety of Northern European wildfowl which over-winter

START & FINISH: *Gartmorn Country Park car park (NS 911940)*

DISTANCE: *5km; 3 miles*

TIME: *1hr 40mins*

MAP: *OS 58*

TERRAIN: *Waymarked paths*

GRADE: *Easy*

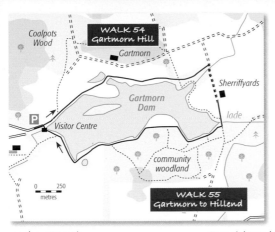

Coalpots Wood

WALK 54
Gartmorn Hill

Gartmorn

Sherriffyards

Gartmorn Dam

lade

P

Visitor Centre

community woodland

WALK 55
Gartmorn to Hillend

0   250
metres

round the north side of the loch to its eastern end, passing a bird hide and the remains of old walls belonging to Sherriffyards Colliery. Most of the coal mines surrounding the loch closed in the 1920s including Sherriffyards and the path on the north side of the loch follows the route of a mineral railway used to transport the coal to Alloa harbour on the Forth.

on the reservoir.

Gartmorn is signposted from the A908 in the village of Sauchie, north of Alloa, and accessed via Schaw Court, which leads to Gartmorn Road and the main car park and Visitor Centre. This walk is the shortest in the area and offers a simple circular route round the loch on tarmac footpaths.

From the car park follow the path

Turn right and follow the track down past the house at Sherriffyards and onto the footpath beyond, which leads to a bridge over the lade feeding the loch from the Black Devon. Turn right here and follow the gravel and tarmac path along the southern side of the loch back to the Visitor Centre.

Access & Parking free

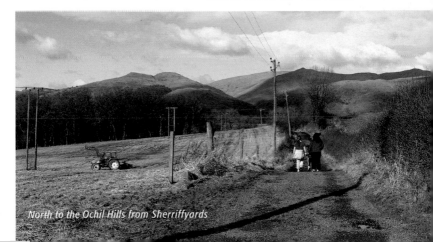

North to the Ochil Hills from Sherriffyards

The Ochils & Gartmorn Dam from
the community woodland

Gartmorn farm and distant Dumyat

*M*oving off the tarmac and gravel paths surrounding Gartmorn Dam offers a slightly wilder walk through Coalpots and Gartmorn Woods to the north of the loch, and Gartmorn Dam Community Woodland to the south.

Both areas have strong connections to coal mining which continued in the area until the late 1970s. The area became a Country Park in 1980, when much of the surrounding land was reclaimed and landscaped. The southern community woodland covers the spoil heaps and remains of mines thought to have been abandoned in the 1870s following flooding and fires.

The northerly woodland grows on land said to have been granted to Henri de Annand by Robert I in 1321. The ancient name Schaw Park to the west of Gartmorn comes from Sir James Schaw, who married Mary de Annand in the 1400s. Some of the original native woodland was planted in the 18th century, while other sections consist of more modern conifers.

From the car park gain the path round the north side of loch. Turn left at the first junction and ascend between fields to a junction with a farm track on the edge of Coalpots Wood. Follow the waymarked path straight ahead into woodland and round to a gate and junction with an access track leading down to Gartmorn Hill Farm. Turn right, then left soon after to enter Gartmornhill Wood and follow the path through this conifer and broadleaf woodland, with glimpses north to the Ochils and south over the farm to the loch.

This brings you out at a four-way junction. Cross straight over onto a

START & FINISH: *Gartmorn Country Park car park (NS 911940)*
DISTANCE: *6km; 3.75 miles*
TIME: *2 hrs*

MAP: *OS 58*
TERRAIN: *Tracks & paths*
GRADE: *Easy / Moderate*

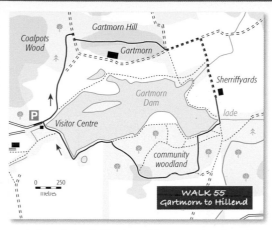

Coalpots Wood

Gartmorn Hill

Gartmorn

Sherriffyards

Gartmorn Dam

lade

P

Visitor Centre

community woodland

0   250
metres

WALK 55
Gartmorn to Hillend

bridge over the lade at the eastern end of the loch.

This marks the start of a network of paths through the community woodland covering the higher ground to the south of the loch. Follow the path around the south side of the loch, before turning left onto a gravel path into the woodland. Ascend to meet a grassy path running along the southern boundary of

track through the fields, then right at the next junction, which leads down to where the continuation of the main route **Around the Loch** [53] comes in from the right. Continue on the track past the house at Sherriffyards and onto a footpath, which leads to a

the plantation to reach a high point with picnic benches overlooking the loch and fine views north to the Ochils. Descend to the loch-side path and follow it back to the car park.

Access & Parking free

North of Sherriffyards

Approaching Hillend

Walkers wishing a longer and more energetic outing can easily combine Gartmorn's paths with the wider path network and connect with the cycle route along the old Alloa to Dumfermline railway south of the Country Park. This is then followed west to the edge of Clackmannan from where farm access roads and tracks can be followed back to the Brothie Burn at the west end of the park.

From the Visitor Centre follow the tarmac lochside path round the north side of Gartmorn Dam loch, passing below Gartmorn Hill Farm and the ruins of Sheriffyard Colliery, to meet the track at the loch's eastern end. Turn right and head down the track past the house at Sherriffyards to where it becomes a footpath. Go over a footbridge and continue straight ahead, signposted to Linn Mill, ignoring the tarmac path which heads off right,

round the southern side of the loch.

Pass over a rise and through a gate from where the track makes a steady descent to cottages at Linn Mill and the main road. Turn right past the entrance to Grassmainston to a Public Footpath on the left, signposted Clackmannan half a mile.

This path leads down through woodland to the Black Devon, which is crossed on a narrow concrete footbridge. Pass below the railway viaduct to steps and a gate which lead up to the tarmac cycleway on the old railway track bed.

Head west towards Clackmannan with its hilltop tower and church and fine views north to the Ochils. Just after passing over a road bridge the tarmac ends and you drop down left to gain the old road alongside, continuing through a gate and past houses to a signpost on the right to Gartmorn

START & FINISH: *Gartmorn Country Park car park (NS 911940)*
DISTANCE: *7.5km; 4.5 miles*
TIME: *2hrs 30mins*

MAP: *OS 58*
TERRAIN: *Roads, tracks & paths*
GRADE: *Easy / Moderate*

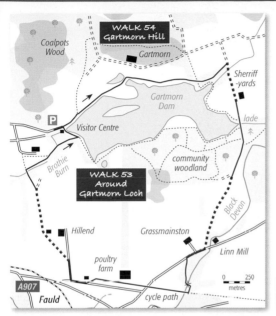

Dam.

Turn right (the old road goes left to the main road), keeping left when the access road divides, and pass a white house on a track which then turns into a footpath. At the gate in the glade, turn right and follow the path beside the Brothie Burn which ascends to old sandstone buildings and concrete steps leading up to the lochside and the circular tarmac path which leads back to the Visitor Centre.

Access & Parking free

Crossing the Black Devon

Dumfries & Galloway

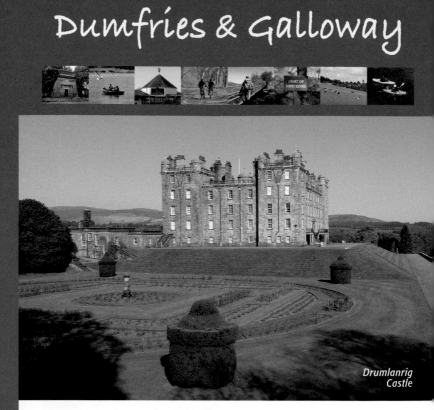

Drumlanrig Castle

Drumlanrig Castle is one of Scotland's great stately homes, with a long and significant history, internationally famous art collection with works by Leonardo, Holbein and Rembrandt and extensive grounds and formal gardens which are fully open to the public.

Commissioned by William Douglas, 1st Duke of Queensberry (who is said never to have lived there), this imposing stately home passed in 1810 to the Scotts, Dukes of Buccleuch, who have lived in and maintained the house and estate ever since.

Outdoor activities are very much encouraged at Drumlanrig with a range of mountain bike routes and waymarked walks through the estate and surrounding countryside and signposted links to paths beside the River Nith and the wider local path network.

Crisscrossed by paths and tracks, **Drumlanrig Woods [56]** date from the 19th century and combine mature deciduous and conifer woodland with more modern plantations and a series of small lochs feeding the Marr Burn. Victorian heather huts, built as summer houses can be found at salient points in the landscape.

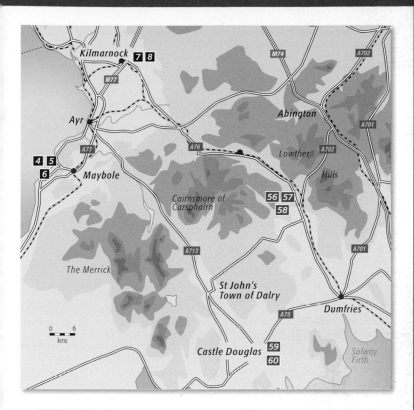

DRUMLANRIG CASTLE COUNTRY ESTATE

Located north-west of Dumfries

Buccleuch Estates
<www.drumlanrig.com>

Getting There

Road: *From Glasgow – M8, M74, A702, minor roads. From Edinburgh – A702, minor roads. From Stirling – M80, M73, M74, A702, minor roads*

Bus: *See p7*

Facilities

Visitor Centre: *(01848 331555), toilets*

Countryside Ranger Service: *Walks & educational events*

Other Activities: *17th century castle & gardens, art & furniture collection, mountain bike courses (bike hire), bicycle museum, canyoning, fishing, adventure playground*

Food, Drink & Shops: *Tearoom, restaurant, cafe, gift shop, plant sales, farmers' market*

The formal gardens and informal parkland to the east of the castle are explored in the **Tree Trail & Bridgeknows Loch** [57] walk. The castle grounds have a number of significant trees including one of the first Douglas firs sent back to Britain in the 1820s by Scottish plant hunter David Douglas to his brother John, who was Drumlanrig Master of Works. Other significant trees are the Drumlanrig Sycamore which dates back to the 18th century and a red oak planted in 1971 by first man on the moon, Neil Armstrong.

The third walk at Drumlanrig is significantly longer than the others and links the castle to the wider path network via signposted paths **Beside the Nith** [58], with a return along a short section of quiet public road.

The Douglas family also has connections with the town of Castle Douglas close to the National Trust for Scotland's Threave Estate, however it is quite a different branch to the Dukes of Queensberry. Castle Douglas is named after farmer's son William Douglas who made his fortune in America before returning to Scotland in the late 18th century as a landowner and industrialist. At that time Castle Douglas was named Carlingwark, as in the adjacent loch. Douglas, now Sir William, had other ideas, getting the village elected a Burgh of Barony and renaming it Castle Douglas. Sir William and 24 members of his family are buried in the mausoleum visited on the walk from **Threave to Carlingwark Loch** [60].

While Castle Douglas can't claim a connection with the most powerful side of the Douglas family, Castle Threave certainly can. This imposing tower house stands on an island in the River Dee and was built following the acquisition in 1369 of the Lordship of Galloway by Archibald, 3rd Earl of Douglas. Archibald was the son of 'The Good Sir James' Douglas, carrier of the heart of Robert I (the Bruce) on crusade against the Moors – see opposite.

Threave House is the centrepiece of the NTS Threave Estate and was built in the 1870s. The estate includes a magnificent formal garden and the now ruined castle, maintained by Historic Scotland. Both can be visited on the final walk round **Threave Castle & Estate** [59].

THREAVE ESTATE

Located at Castle Douglas

National Trust for Scotland
<www.nts.org.uk>

Getting There
Road: From Glasgow – M8, M74, A701, A75. From Edinburgh – A702, M74, A701, A75. From Stirling – M80, M73, M74, A701, A75.

Bus: See p7

Facilities
Visitor Centre: (0844 4932245), toilets

Countryside Ranger Service: Walks & educational events

Other Activities: 19th century baronial house & gardens, sculpture trail, wildfowl reserve (bird hides), countryside centre, Threave Castle (Historic Scotland)

Food, Drink & Shops: Restaurant, gift shop, plant sales

Sir James Douglas is said to have carried the heart of Robert I (the Bruce) in a silver casket on crusade against the Moors in Spain, in fulfilment of the monarch's dying wish. The Douglas motto 'Forward, Brave Heart' is represented by the winged heart on this sign near Castle Douglas. The motto is also that of the Douglases of Drumlanrig Castle. Douglas also earned the nickname 'Black Douglas' from his raids on England.

Beech Loch

Drumlanrig is surrounded by extensive park and woodland offering a number of fine walks on waymarked and signposted paths. The 'Pink Palace' as it is often known on account of its red sandstone was commissioned in 1679 by William Douglas, the 1st Duke of Queensberry.

The 2nd duke was the notorious 'Union Duke' whose Machiavellian political skills benefitted Scotland during negotiations on the 1707 Act of Union, while the 4th duke led a debauched life in London and is said to have cut down most of the surrounding woodlands. When he died without an heir the castle and title passed to Henry Scott, 3rd Duke of Buccleuch. It remains the family home of the current Duke of Buccleuch and Queensberry. This walk explores the castle's woodland largely replanted by Walter, 5th Duke of Buccleuch, and subsequent generations.

Gain the track which starts from the main car park and follow it uphill away from the castle, to just past a house on the left. Turn left at a telegraph pole and go straight up the grass to a wooden gate into woodland at the top. The path beyond leads to a track which is followed round to the right, keeping left when it divides. Continue to a four-way junction and turn left down a grassy ride, then right at a post onto a path. This leads through woodland,

The hut at Butts Knowe

START & FINISH: *Drumlanrig Castle car park (NX 852994)*

DISTANCE: *4.5km; 2.75 miles*

TIME: *1hr 30mins*

MAP: *OS 78*

TERRAIN: *Tracks & paths; some signs & waymarks*

GRADE: *Easy*

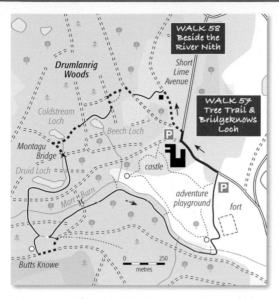

either of these but turn right and ascend to the heather-clad summer house at Butts Knowe which can be seen up among the trees ahead. Continue past the summer house to exit onto a track. Follow it left and over the burn and down to a junction with another track.

Turn left – Mountain Bike Route (MTB) 7 – and follow the track down. At a right-hand bend keep a look out for a path on the left and follow it back to the junction with the bench. If you have

then swings rightwards round Beech Loch to exit onto a track.

Cross straight over – signposted for Coldstream and Hillhead Lochs – and follow a waymarked track, keeping left at a junction to gain the end of Coldstream Loch. Turn left at the next junction – signposted right to Hillhead Loch – and descend the track to the stone Montagu Bridge.

From the bridge gain a path on the left-hand side of the burn and follow it down towards the Druid Loch and main access road. Turn right before the access road and follow the loch to exit onto the road further along. Cross straight over, continue to a footbridge over a burn and ascend to a junction and a bench. One waymarked route continues straight on and one continues down to the left. Don't take

descended to a point where a waymarked route goes off right then you have gone too far. From the bench turn right and follow the path down and over a track to the Marr Burn and another track with St Geoffrey's Bridge on the left. Continue past a footbridge, with glimpses through the trees to the castle and the Marr Cascade to another footbridge with a gate.

Pass some picnic benches and over another footbridge to gates. These give access to the garden, but are locked from 4.30pm. Continue on and through a kissing gate then up and over the site of a Roman fort to the Adventure Playground car park and access road. Follow the road up left path the castle to the main car park.

Access & Parking charge

Bridgeknows Loch

*H*ardly a castle in the traditional sense, Drumlanrig straddles the period in which castles metamorphosed from fortified dwellings to stately mansions. Robert Adam's magnificent **Culzean Castle [4, 5, 6]** dates from the same period. The style reached its peak in the late 1800s with Scottish Baronial country houses such as **Threave [59, 60]**.

Originally laid out in the 1700s, the gardens at Drumlanrig have undergone many changes over the centuries, most recently during the last war when the cultivation of food took precedence over shrubs and flowers. Over the past 70 years the gardens have been fully restored to reflect different ages and designs, both formal and informal.

The gardens also house a variety of trees both ancient and modern. These have been linked to make a Tree Trail which forms part of this walk, as does

a modern adventure playground and some of the wood and thatch summer houses built in the 1840s.

Before starting this walk it is worth investigating the Stableyard opposite the car park. The Scottish Cycle Museum can be found here and more

Drumlanrig sycamore

START & FINISH: *Drumlanrig Castle car park (NX 852994)*

DISTANCE: *4km; 2.5 miles*

TIME: *1hr 20mins*

MAP: *OS 78*

TERRAIN: *Tracks & paths; some signs & waymarks*

GRADE: *Easy*

than 70 cycles ranging from a replica of Kirkpatrick Macmillan's 1840 velocipede to a penny farthing and a modern mountain bike. Macmillan was an apprentice at the castle before becoming blacksmith at Keir Mill to the south, where he is credited with adding pedals for propulsion to the existing two-wheeled cycle to produce the modern bicycle.

Return to the car park, continue past the stables and through a white gate into the garden. Take the first right following the Tree Trail signs and soon after on the left is an American red oak planted in 1971 by first man on the moon, Neil Armstrong. Continue following the signs, descending past one of the largest weeping beeches in Britain, then turning right and ascending to the summer house overlooking one of the first Douglas Firs planted in Britain. Scottish plant hunter David Douglas sent the seeds for this giant to his brother John, Master of Works at Drumlanrig.

Descend steps still following the Tree Trail signs left, then right to come out onto the formal lawns in front of the castle. Drop down to the right and follow a path above the Marr Burn past a bridge, then ascend away from the burn and round to another summer house. Beyond that, follow the path round left to a junction where the Tree Trail goes sharp left.

Continue straight ahead at this point to pass the adventure playground and exit right to the car park. Turn left and follow the access road towards the castle and an information board on the right about the 300-year old Drumlanrig sycamore. Cross over to the sycamore then veer right over parkland to gain a track and follow it to just

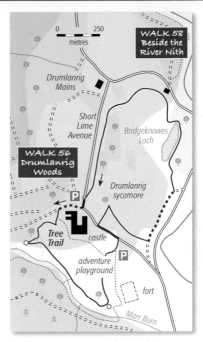

before it descends to the road.

Leave the track and ascend left of the fenced woodland to reach Bridgeknowes Loch. Follow the path round its right side past picnic tables then swing round to the left across pasture towards Drumlanrig Mains farm and the Short Lime Avenue. The newer lime trees here were planted to commemorate Queen Elizabeth's 1977 Silver Jubilee, the older ones by the 3rd Duke of Queensbury.

Either follow the avenue or the pasture and parkland immediately west of it, back to the car park.

Access & Parking charge

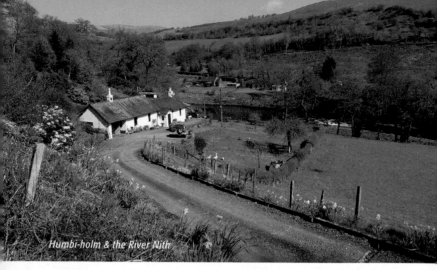

Humbi-holm & the River Nith

*N*orth of Drumlanrig Castle a long section of the River Nith can be followed to Glenairlie, with a return south along a short section of quiet country road to a waymarked track leading back to the riverside.

The southern section is characterised by conifer woodland with views over the Nith with its rocky linns, the northern section by open farmland increasingly enclosed by grassy hillsides. It's quite a long walk, although the route and terrain are straightforward, the only uphill of any note coming at the start of the return along the minor road to Sweetbit.

Parking is possible at Drumlanrig Castle (charges apply but there are toilets, a cafe and much more), at Drumlanrig Bridge at the start of the castle approach road and opposite the white house a short distance north of the bridge, where a track leads down to the river.

From the main castle car park gain a track parallel to but below the tree-lined drive, and follow it through pasture down and right towards the

River Nith

START & FINISH: *Drumlanrig Castle car park (NX 852994)*
DISTANCE: *18km; 11.25 miles*
TIME: *5hrs 30mins*

MAP: *OS 78*
TERRAIN: *Roads, tracks & paths; mostly signposted*
GRADE: *Moderate*

white cottage on the access road. Gain the track opposite the cottage and follow it towards to the river and a white gate. Drop down right before the gate to a pedestrian gate and a path through broadleaf woodland above the Nith. The scenery here is very beautiful, with the rocks of the Nith Linns generating areas of white water in the gorge below.

The path ascends back to the main track, Queen's Drive, which leads into the narrow constraints of the gorge where it shares space with the river, road and railway to gain more open country again and a four-way track junction overlooking the house at Humbi-holm. Continue straight ahead (the return route comes down the track on the left) onto a grassy path signposted Glenairlie and follow this into conifer plantations.

Descend to the edge of the woodland and a gate and exit into open rough riverside grazing. Here the path leads back to the river, becomes a track and passes through fields to swing round left and down to the road beyond Burnmouth farm.

Turn left here and follow the road uphill to a Y-junction and a house. Keep left and continue ascending to good views north to the steep-sided Dalveen Pass and Lowther Hill with its radar 'golf ball' beyond. Pass the entrance to Crairiepark and on through woodland to where the road swings right and passes Crairiehill. Sweetbit cottage surrounded by high pine trees lies ahead, but turn left before then onto a track to Sweetbit farm, signposted Nith Linns.

The farm is skirted on the left, following the signs, from where a quiet tree-lined lane leads down to the four-

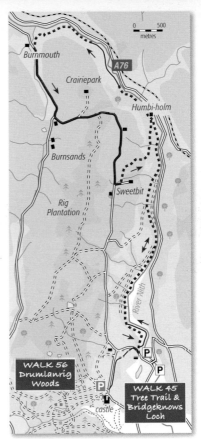

way junction at Humbi-holm. Turn right and follow the Queen's Drive back to the start. Keep an ear out for mountain bikers as the track forms part of the extensive network of waymarked mountain bike routes on the Drumlanrig estate.

Access & Parking charge

Threave Castle & the River Dee

Situated beside the River Dee on the outskirts of Castle Douglas, this large estate offers a variety of outdoor activities including an interesting walk linking a newly restored Victorian country house and gardens, with an extensive wildfowl reserve and the ruins of imposing Threave Castle.

The walk can be tackled in two stages, divided by a welcome lunch break in the National Trust for Scotland (NTS) Visitor Centre cafe: starting with the longer Estate Walk and ending with a more leisurely wander round Threave House and Gardens in the afternoon.

From the main Visitor Centre car park walk a short way back along the access road, then left down the grass bank (signposted Estate Walk) to a lower access road. Turn left then right and through the Estate Walk car park and cross over the main road past Hightae Cottage to a track.

A parallel woodland path is gained and

leads down to houses where you swing round on an access road to reach steps on the right just before the main road. These lead round to the main road opposite a gated track. Cross over and follow the track up and over the A75 to a pedestrian gate up on the right, which gives access to Barley Hill wood and views over to Castle Douglas. Where the path joins the old railway line turn left and follow it to just beyond the bridge where a path leads up right to join the road to Threave Castle.

A signposted path leads from the white-washed farmhouse and outbuildings of

Threave sculpture trail

START & FINISH: *Threave Estate car park (NX 753607)*
DISTANCE: 9km; 5.5 miles
TIME: 3hrs (ex. house & garden)

MAP: *OS 84*
TERRAIN: *Roads, tracks & paths; some waymarks*
GRADE: *Easy / Moderate*

NTS Threave Wildfowl Reserve to the castle. Maintained and opened to the public by Historic Scotland, Threave Castle stands on an island in the middle of the Dee and is reached by small boat during the summer months, the entry charge including the short boat trip. Built in the late 1300s by Scotland's most powerful nobles, the Earls of Douglas, it's the oldest and biggest tower house in the region and Scotland's only castle in a river.

Retrace your steps to the old railway and turn right towards Lamb Island, exiting onto the access road to Lodge of Kelton farm. Follow the access road left past houses and straight ahead onto a track and bridge over the A75.

Kelton Mains

Turn left soon after and follow the sometimes muddy path through woodland and fields, crossing a minor road and continuing on to another. Turn left here and follow the road back to Hightae Cottage and the car park.

Threave House and Gardens offer a relaxing wander round a garden best known for its 200 varieties of springtime daffodils. A sculpture trail can be followed from the walled garden through formal and informal gardens to Threave House itself. Restored to 1930s grandeur, the principle rooms of this baronial-style country house were first opened to the public in 2002. From the top right-hand corner of the garden a path leads round the upper wood down to the car park.

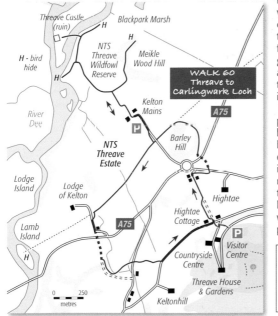

> Estate Access & Parking free
> Charge for access to Threave Castle, House & Gardens

Carlingwark Loch & Castle Douglas

Built for Liverpool merchant William Gordon in 1872, Threave House was designed by architect Charles Kinnear, one of the leading proponents of the Scottish Baronial-Style with its asymmetrical elevations, corbelled turrets and stepped gables.

Threave, however, has the added innovation of a large balustraded tower via which the house is entered, followed by a grand main staircase giving direct access to the principal rooms on the first and second floors. The house and estate were given to the National Trust for Scotland (NTS) by Alan Gordon in 1948 and the main rooms opened to the public in 2002 after refurbishment to what they would have looked like in the 1930s.

The gardens have long sustained the Trust's School of Practical Gardening and the estate also boasts Scotland's

first-ever dedicated bat reserve. A Bat Trail and 'Bat Mobile' explore some of the favourite roosts of the seven species of bats found on the estate.

Explore the house, gardens and countryside centre at will before making a circular tour of Kelton Hill Wood, which can be accessed from a gate at the top right corner of the garden, and return

Threave House

START & FINISH: *Threave Estate car park (NX 753607)*

DISTANCE: *12km; 7.5 miles*

TIME: *4hrs (inc. house & gardens)*

MAP: *OS 84 (NX 753607)*

TERRAIN: *Roads, tracks & paths; some signposts*

GRADE: *Easy / Moderate*

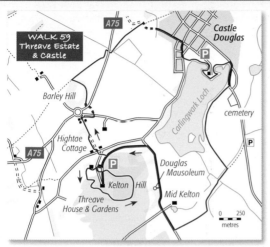

to the main Visitor Centre car park. The house and gardens are about 3km of the total distance given for this walk.

Walk a short way back along the access road, then left down the grass bank (signposted Estate Walk) to a lower access road. Turn left then right and through the Estate Walk car park and cross over the main road past Hightae Cottage to a track.

A parallel woodland path is gained and leads down to houses where you swing round on an access road to reach steps on the right just before the main road. These lead round to the main road opposite a gated track. Cross over and follow the track up and over the A75 to a pedestrian gate up on the right, which gives access to Barley Hill wood and views to Castle Douglas.

Descend to the railway path and go right, follow the Castle Douglas signpost right through fields towards the main road. Pass under the roadbridge over the river, then cross the river to

regain the track bed of the former railway and follow it to an old road leading into Castle Douglas.

Turn right at the High Street and follow it to Carlingwark Loch. Cross over to gain the lochside path which leads round past Carlingwark Outdoor Activity Centre back to the road. The lochside path, known as Lovers Walk, starts again further along on the right and follows the east side of the loch past a bird hide to a junction with a path coming in from the left. Boardwalks now lead rightwards through an area of marsh marked by reeds and rushes until they end and a narrow path leads between fields to exit at a road.

Turn right and follow the road to Mid Kelton. The road isn't busy, but there are some blind bends and no pavement, so care is needed. Pass the parish church and the Egyptian style Douglas Mausoleum which holds the remains of 25 members of the Douglas family including William Douglas who in 1792 had Carlingwark Village created a Burgh of Barony and renamed Castle Douglas.

The road soon leads back to the entrance to Threave and the access road to the car park.

Estate Access & Parking free
Charge for access to Threave
House & Gardens (NTS)

mica *walkers' guides*

Available from all good high street and internet bookshops
www.micapublishing.com